Italian Cooking

BY POPPY CANNON

GROSSET
GOOD LIFE
BOOKS

PUBLISHERS • GROSSET & DUNLAP • NEW YORK
A FILMWAYS COMPANY

Acknowledgments

Cover photograph by Mort Engel

The author wishes to express her appreciation for permission to use the drawings and photographs by the following: Joyce Biegeleisen: p. 8, p. 22, p. 42, p. 45 top, p. 46, p. 48, p. 53, p. 63, p. 64, p. 65, p. 67 top; Jane Mutshnick: p. 5, p. 7, p. 11, p. 12 bottom, p. 13, p. 16 top, p. 18 bottom, p. 23, p. 27, p. 28, p. 38, p. 41, p. 50, p. 51, p. 52, p. 55, p. 58, p. 60, p. 66, p. 71, p. 72 top, p. 73 top, p. 75, p. 76; ENIT: p. 10, p. 25, p. 33, p. 47, p. 59, p. 62, p. 70, p. 77; Alexis Gregory (photographs courtesy Fratelli Fabbri Editori, Milan): p. 12 top, p. 16 bottom, p. 18 top, p. 21, p. 32, p. 37, p. 39, p. 40, p. 45 bottom, p. 54, p. 67 buttom, p. 68, p. 72, p. 73.

1976 Printing

Copyright © 1975 by Grosset & Dunlap, Inc.
All rights reserved
Published simultaneously in Canada
Library of Congress catalog card number: 75-5427
ISBN 0-448-12053-4 (trade edition)
ISBN 0-448-13320-2 (library edition)

Printed in the United States of America

Contents

1 Setting the Scene   5
2 Appetizers and First Courses   7
3 Soups   15
4 Seafood   20
5 Meats and Poultry   26
6 Eggs, Rice, and Cheeses   36
7 Vegetables   44
8 Pasta   49
9 Salads   57
10 Pizza, Heroes, Sandwiches, and Bread   61
11 Dessert and Coffee   69
   Index   78

1
Setting the Scene

Of all the cuisines of the world Italian is probably the closest of all to the American heart and palate. Right now, across the country, the pizza may be far more American than apple pie. Americans are waking up, as well, to the grand simplicities of Italian cooking.

Almost without realizing it we have become Italy-oriented. Even in top-flight gourmet circles, it is admissible to prefer Italian, and particularly North Italian, cuisine to all but the most inimitable French.

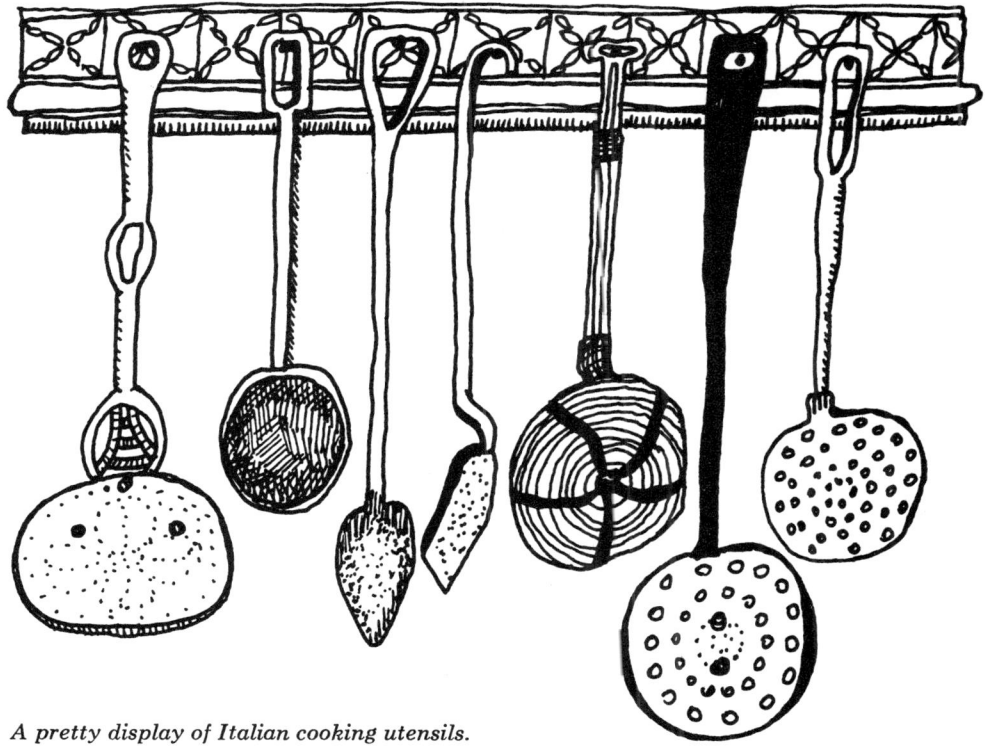

A pretty display of Italian cooking utensils.

Americans, like Italians, prefer food close to its natural state. As one man phrased it, "I want it to taste like what it is, gone to heaven."

The Italians, unlike the French, have no fetish about the importance of long cookery. There are legends in this country about long-simmered spaghetti sauces, but these are relatively few in number. Essentially, the Italians and the Americans are devotees of quick cookery, though for very different reasons.

Often the Italian cook spends most of the waking hours in some aspect of cookery. Many Italian housewives shop twice a day, sometimes to insure freshness, at other times for the sake of economy—to take advantage of day-end bargains.

But, even in the smallest, most out-of-the-way American town, a few easily obtainable staples can introduce quickly, easily, and seductively some of the joys of Italian cooking—even to those who have never before turned a hand to the skillet.

The gourmets may achieve the ultimate dream of May in Rome when the first piselli and prosciutto appear not only at the great restaurants but at the little trattorias off the Via Veneto. For we now have in frozen packages the most infant little green peas in the world, no bigger than grains of caviar; and we can buy Italian prosciutto almost anywhere—not exactly like Roman, perhaps, but enough, and with much of the savor as well as the look of scrapings off giant garnets.

In any discussion of Italian food we must first get rid of certain ingrained preconceptions. Italian food is not all spaghetti and other pastas. In Venice, for example, people much prefer rice. They do not subsist entirely on scaloppine or even on veal. Chicken is often much easier to get. In any small town you simply ask a neighbor to place some eggs for you under a setting hen, and later, when the time comes, return the favor.

All Italy does not consume quantities of garlic. Basil, oregano, and rosemary are even more popular in many sections. Tomato sauce is only one of hundreds of well known *salse* (sauces). All Italian cooking is not done with olive oil. In the past this was true, but now various other vegetable oils are replacing olive oil because they are far more economical and more durable.

As for pizzas, they can be found where they originated, in Naples, and there are pizzerias in Rome and other large cities, although they are often considered an American innovation. This, however, should make them no less attractive to the American palate.

Except for China and France, there is no country in the world where the food is so varied. Italy is the land of honest cooking, and yet it is appealingly sophisticated.

Epicures who have toured the world write and speak lyrically of the great variety of vegetables in Italy and the exquisite manner in which they are cooked so that they stay crisp and natural. Although they do not use the wok, Italians often make use of the Chinese stir-fry method for cooking spinach and other greens. Many of their egg dishes, and particularly their frittati, are similar to the pancake omelets of the Orient. Outside of the large cities in the United States, most Italian restaurants are run by Sicilians or Neapolitans. So for many Americans, much of Italian cookery comes as something of a shock.

In this book we have introduced a number of new techniques of cooking pasta, for instance, and polenta, in fast, foolproof ways. These methods are made possible by a different type of processing. The perfectionists will no doubt be shocked by our use of canned and processed foods but we have tried to provide a guide to the best available.

We hope that you will find here a trove of ideas for planned as well as unplanned—and certainly interesting—menus, even for hurried and otherwise harassed occasions.

2
Appetizers and First Courses

Antipasto Simplicity

Usually before lunch, and quite often at a meal where a pasta will not be the introduction to the repast, a selection of tidbits is proffered. They can be selections of whatever happens to be handy. This one is particularly appetizing. We will not give amounts because so much depends upon what happens to be available.

    Cole slaw
    Onion rings (white or red)
    Salami slices
    Sliced hard-boiled eggs
        with capers

    Pickled beets
    Sardines
    Pimentoes
    Olives (black, green; stuffed, unstuffed)

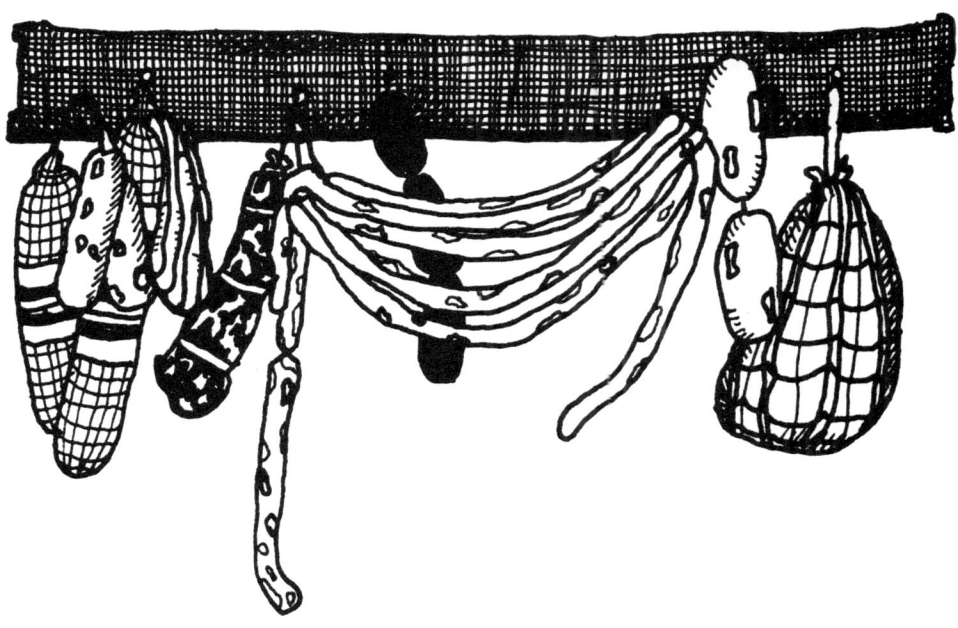

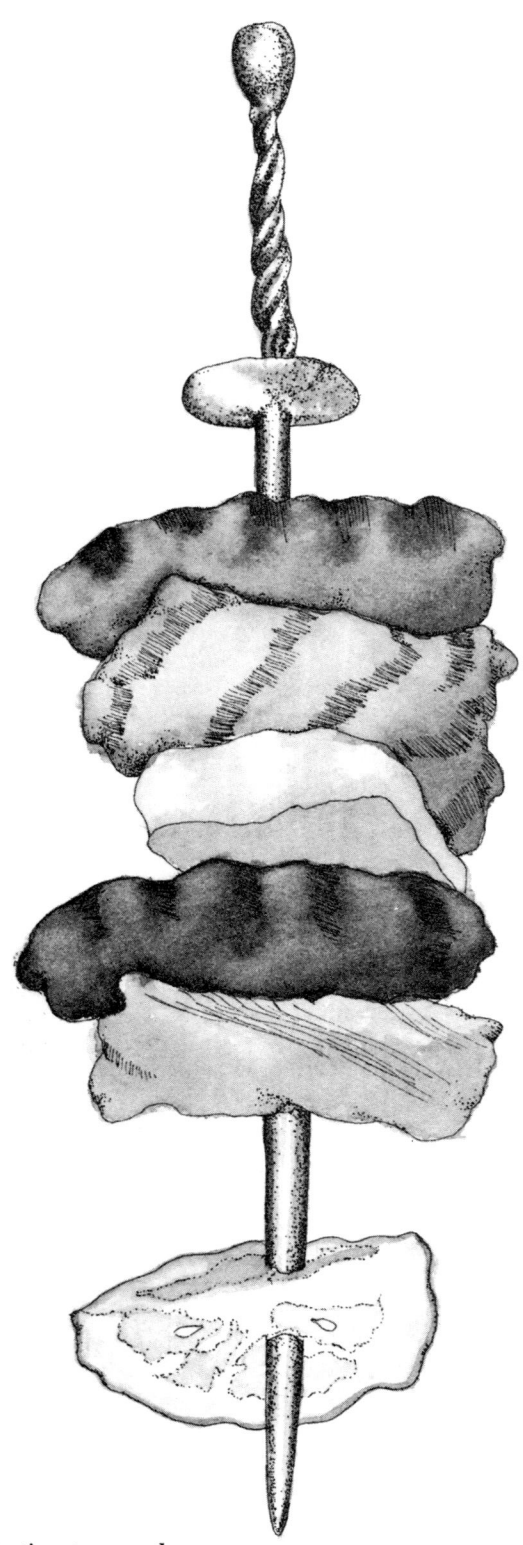

Antipasto on a skewer.

In America antipasto is often served with an oil-and-vinegar dressing mixed with chopped onion and chopped parsley; however, it is far more authentic merely to present vials of wine vinegar and olive oil. For those who want to be more truly Italian, sections of lemon may be used instead of the vinegar.

Antipasto Tipico

This amount will serve two. Multiply as you will.

4 thin slices Italian salami	8 large green olives
4 thin slices prosciutto	2 tsp. capers
4 anchovy fillets	4 artichoke hearts in oil
2 celery hearts, cut in halves lengthwise	4 small tomatoes
1 small can tuna fish	4 pickled peppers
	5 black olives

Arrange on individual plates or large platters and pass the olive oil and vinegar for those who want it. With a cup of broth, some crusty bread, wine, fruit, and cheese, this makes a fine supper.

Bagna Cauda
Hot Bath for Raw Vegetables

In the Piedmont area of Italy and especially around the vicinity of Turin they have a specialty that was formerly considered almost a national dish. Translated, it might be called a hot dip. The name actually means hot bath. Essentially it is peasant eating. All sorts of raw vegetables—celery, endive, sweet peppers, raw artichokes, fennel—almost any vegetables that are crisp and edible raw—are dipped into *bagna cauda,* a golden, simmering pool of richness which combines butter and olive oil, garlic, anchovies, and, upon occasion, slivers of the white truffles that come from and around the little town of Alba.

In the northern wine lands, this dish is not an appetizer but a whole meal, for it is served with bread and cheese and the sturdy, usually red wines of the land.

Often in the northern cities of Italy—at Giannino's in Milan, for example—they serve *bagna cauda* along with their famous boiled beef. It is, of course, also good on all kinds of vegetables, raw and cooked. In our day and age it has already been taken up by resourceful hostesses who are weary of the usual sour-cream dips at cocktail parties.

Being quite rich with oil and butter, it is very important that it be served a-simmering. An electric hot tray or candle warmer will do the job admirably.

In Italy, each person gets his own portion of *bagna cauda*, but here at our gatherings we would probably use it as a communal dip, in much the same way fondue is served.

6 or 8 garlic cloves	1 white truffle
¾ cup Italian olive oil	(optional)
1 cup butter	1 Tbs. cream
12 anchovy fillets, coarsely chopped	(optional)

Put the garlic through a press, then blend with the olive oil; or blend with the olive oil in an electric blender. Combine the butter with the oil and garlic mixture. Heat all together until the butter is melted and the oil is hot. Add the anchovy fillets. If you should be lucky enough to have access to a white truffle, cut it into very thin slivers or chop it fine and add to the *bagna cauda*.

(Some cooks like to stir in a tablespoonful of cream, in which case they use less butter and more olive oil.) Do not boil but keep the *bagna cauda* warm for about 20 minutes in order to blend and mellow the flavors.

Bring to the table in the dish in which it was made and keep hot in a chafing dish or earthenware casserole, over a candle warmer, spirit lamp, or an electric hot tray.

In its homeland the *bagna cauda* is often accompanied in proper season by *topinambùr*, which is Jerusalem artichoke (a relative of the potato) or cardoon. Actually, it is the root of the sunflower.

Provide an attractive assortment of raw vegetables, including, if possible, bunches of Belgian endive that has been cut lengthwise into quarters; also celery, carrot sticks, strips of sweet red or green peppers, green onions, raw small artichokes, cauliflowerets, or whatever you wish.
Makes 3 cups.

Carpaccio

Several Italian restaurateurs claim credit for having invented Manhattan's latest fad, a new version of steak tartare, *carpaccio*. Credit, however, we believe, should go to Harry's Bar in Venice.

Our own quick new version is nothing more than much-parsleyed mayonnaise-plus. Readied in moments, *carpaccio* (meaning capers in Italian) is a luscious, impressive first course using slices of raw round or tenderloin steak served flat and cut very thin, with a wide ribbon of the sauce spread over all.

1½ lbs. thin as thin leanest round or tenderloin steak (about 18 paper-thin slices)	½ cup parsley leaves
	2 Tbs. vinegar or lemon juice
	1 Tbs. capers
	4 sour gherkins
½ small white onion, cut up	4 anchovy fillets
	4 tsp. prepared Dijon mustard
1 clove garlic, halved	1 cup mayonnaise

To make sauce: Put vinegar or lemon juice into blender with capers, gherkins, anchovies, onion, garlic, mustard, parsley. Blend about 40 seconds. Add mayonnaise and whir 5 seconds longer. Makes about 1½ cups sauce.

To serve, arrange 3 slices of steak on each plate and draw a wide ribbon of sauce across the center of the plate. Or, if you wish, sauce may be served separately.
Serves 6.

Carrots Marinotti

Fresh carrot sticks cut into 2-inch lengths are classic for this delicious country appetizer but leftover cooked carrots may also be used. It is important, however, that the carrots should not have been overcooked, because they will need to stand in a dressing for several hours and may become too soft. The marinade consists of olive oil, red wine vinegar, and oregano plus garlic. We have had very good results using Italian bottled dressing, diet or otherwise.

1 small clove garlic	¼ tsp. dried marjoram or oregano
2 cups cooked carrots	(or ½ tsp. fresh)
1 cup bottled Italian dressing	

Appetizers and First Courses

Lightly crush the garlic and bury in a mound of the carrots. Add marjoram or oregano and pour on enough Italian dressing to cover but not swim. Cover and chill from half an hour to 24 hours.

This is one of the thrifty vegetable salads that often go on to a luncheon antipasto. If served alone, it should be ringed with interesting greenery such as rugola, watercress, escarole, or even ribbons of young green cabbage. Serves 4 to 6.

Insalata Céci

One of the many vegetable salads that appear as a first course is made of *céci*, or chickpeas (known in Spanish-speaking areas as *garbanzos*). These beans take very well to canning but should be well rinsed in cold water, chilled, and dried before being mixed with the salad dressing. Lima beans may be substituted for the *céci*.

1 can cooked *céci* or lima beans
1 can or 2 cups cooked sliced carrots
Italian dressing
1 can pimientos, drained
Celery hearts or *finocchio* (fennel)
Olives for garnish

To serve, arrange beans and carrots in separate mounds on a platter. Garnish with pimientos and hearts of celery or *finocchio* and olives. Serve chilled, along with the meat course or as a first course.

Crab Meat Grand Canal

The crab meat served on the Grand Canal in Venice is different from ours. It comes in large, sunset-orange shells that are often used as serving dishes for the appetizer. Any sort of

The grand canal of Venice.

seashells may be substituted; and if fresh-cooked little chunks—not shreds—of crab meat are unavailable, use frozen. For economy, tuna fish or albacore (what most people consider white tuna fish) may be substituted.

1½ lbs. frozen crab meat lumps	2 Tbs. very light olive oil
3 Tbs. lemon juice	Leaves of fennel, celery, or watercress for garnish
Black pepper	

If you have time, thaw the crab meat in the refrigerator overnight. To use immediately, place the pliofilm packets in a saucepan and add cold water to cover. Bring quickly, uncovered, to a boil. Remove immediately and place the bag under cold running water. The crab meat will be thawed and cool.

Divide crab meat into 6 portions. Pile on shells or in champagne glasses. Sprinkle with lemon juice. Place a few grinds of black pepper all over each portion. Dribble with olive oil.

Usually each person does his own tossing but you may do the preparation ahead of time if you like and then serve the crab meat garnished with sprays of fennel leaves, celery leaves, or watercress.
Serves 6.

Crustini

Antipasto literally means before the meal, but it has taken on a far different connotation in Italy. Actually an antipasto, even in some fine restaurants like the Trattoria in New York, is a buffet providing the whole meal with hot as well as cold entrées. Miniature pizzas are included among hot *antipasti;* so are *crustini.*

Cut white bread into squares or circles. Remove crusts. Toast lightly on one side. Brush untoasted side with olive oil. Cover with provolone or any other tasty white cheese, crisscross with fillets of anchovy and set under broiler just long enough to melt but not harden the cheese.

Finocchio
Fennel

Finocchio is a celery-type vegetable with frondlike leaves that resemble dill. Both the firm, bulbous flesh and the leaves have a surprising, and for many people, an enchanting flavor of anise.

Generally it is cut into wedges, more or less like celery hearts, and served plain. Only a few people insist on salt.

Many Italians, however, do not serve *finocchio* at the beginning of the meal but reserve it as a kind of special savory for the end of a rich repast.

Sometimes an Italian grocer will give you a sly smile when you ask for *finocchio* because, like many other ordinary words—tomato, fruit, pansy, poule—it has another meaning. Literally *finocchio* means "fine eyes," and the word goes back to the ancient feasts of Lucullus and perhaps even further back to the Greeks and the Babylonians when pretty boys were brought out to entertain the sated guests.

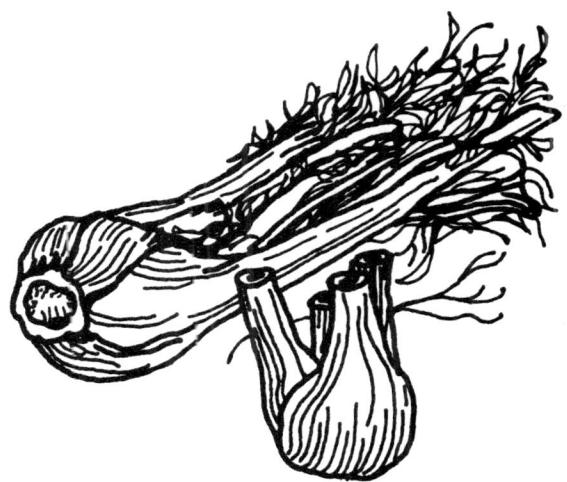

Finocchio.

Mozzarella in Carrozza
Cheese in a Carriage

This is a type of deep-fried cheese sandwich. In different parts of Italy it is made in different ways: fried in olive oil in the south, in butter or lard in the north.

Sometimes, especially when the little carriages are served as an hors d'oeuvre, the bread is cut into attractive shapes.

As an appetizer this specialty is served hot. As a picnic snack it is eaten at room temperature. Any mild, creamy white cheese may be substituted for mozzarella. The cheese and the bread should be about the same size and almost the same thickness. You need twice as many slices of bread as of cheese.

8 thin slices white bread	½ cup (about) fine bread crumbs or flour
8 slices mozzarella cheese, about ¼ inch thick	2 eggs
	½ tsp. salt
½ cup (about) milk	1 cup (about) butter, olive oil, or lard

Cut the crusts off the bread and cut the slices in halves, making 16 pieces. Place the cheese between the slices of bread, making a sandwich. Dip the edges of the sandwich in milk and then in bread crumbs or flour. Or roll the whole sandwich in flour after dipping the edges in milk.

Beat eggs slightly with the salt. Dip entire sandwich into beaten eggs.

Heat olive oil, butter, or lard in a 5-inch frying pan to about 350°F. If you use a larger frying pan, use more fat. It should stand about an inch deep—enough to cover the sandwich completely. Fry not more than 2 or 3 pieces at a time until pale gold. If necessary, you may turn the sandwich with a spatula or two forks. Remove from pan and drain on paper towels.

This recipe makes 16 "carriages." The pieces may be cut into halves or even thirds to serve as appetizers. You may find it a little difficult to cut the "carriages" while they are still hot. Do it before cooking or after cooling.

Mozzarella in carrozza.

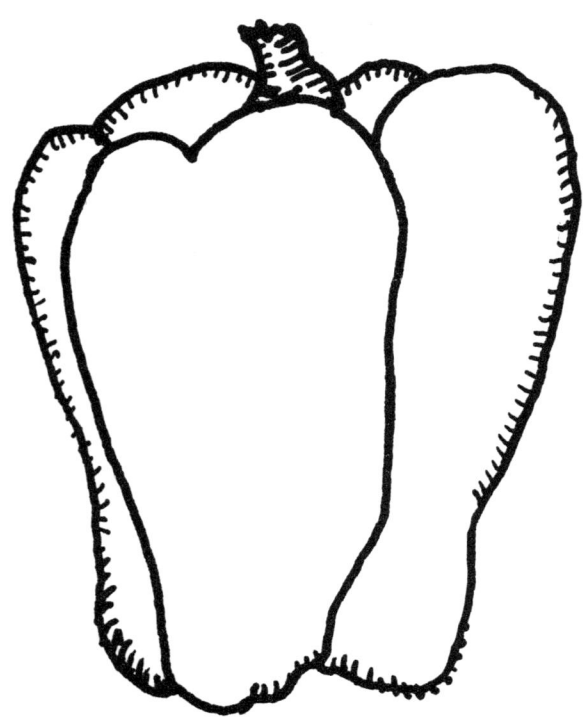

Broiled Peppers and Anchovies

Sweet peppers—green, red, and sometimes even yellow—are to be found in most markets all year round. Since this dish is so savory and goes so fast after you get started on it, we are giving the recipe to make 8 or 10 antipasto servings.

8 or 10 medium-size sweet peppers	4 large garlic cloves
16 to 20 anchovy fillets	Freshly ground pepper
4 Tbs. capers	2 cups (about) olive oil
¼ tsp. oregano	

Place the peppers, whole, under a hot broiler

12   *Italian Cooking*

and char lightly on both sides till skin is blistered and blackened, but not burned.

Instead of burning your fingers trying to skin the hot peppers as most cookbooks suggest, do what they do in the old country. Simply put them in the sink under running cold water and rub a little so that the charred skin comes off and the tiny bits go down the drain. Cut the denuded peppers lengthwise into 1-inch strips. Remove all the seeds and pulpy inner core. Pat dry with paper towels.

In a wide, shallow serving dish arrange the pepper strips in 4 or 5 layers, topping each layer with about 4 anchovy fillets, cut in halves crosswise. Sprinkle each layer also with 1 tablespoon of capers and a pinch of oregano. Over each layer crush a clove of garlic, put through the press, and add pepper to taste. Add just enough olive oil to cover. Cover dish tightly with foil and set in the refrigerator for at least half an hour or for several days, if you wish.

If you serve this dish directly from the refrigerator, serve with warmed, crusty bread. If allowed to come to room temperature before serving, bread may be cold.
Serves 8 or 10.

Tomatoes Stuffed with Artichoke Hearts

Although in Italy artichoke hearts are sold fresh, ready prepared for cooking, I have never found them in this country except inside the artichoke. But they are widely available here frozen—plain or buttered—and in cans and jars—in brine, oil, or pickled. Considering the fact that they are such a delicacy, the price, while high, is not exorbitant. And they are most impressive. You may, however, substitute pickled mushrooms for the artichoke hearts.

6 large tomatoes	½ cup commercial sour cream
Salt and pepper	
Pinch of dill	½ tsp. lemon juice mixed with grated onion to taste
6 artichoke hearts, frozen or canned	
1 cup mayonnaise	¼ tsp. curry powder

Skin the tomatoes. Scoop out centers and season inside and out with salt, pepper, and a pinch of dill. Place an artichoke heart cooked

according to package directions—or 2 or 3 pickled mushrooms—inside each tomato. Chill. Half an hour before serving, mix together the mayonnaise, sour cream, curry powder, and lemon juice and grated onion, and spoon over the tomatoes.

Like many other Italian appetizers or first courses, these may be served as a main dish at lunch or supper.
Serves 6 as a first course.

Melon or Figs with Prosciutto

In July, when the melons and the green figs appear, and in August, when the purple figs are ripe, Italian gourmets give up all other forms of appetizers in favor of these fruits served with the thinnest possible slices of ham. The renowned hams of Parma are considered most appropriate, but many types of smoky, long-cured Italian *prosciutti* are used. In the vicinity of Bologna, known for centuries as the home of excellent pork sausage, pungent salami often takes the place of ham. No matter how peppery the meat, a mill filled with peppercorns is always on hand.

Domestic prosciutto (much of it made in Hoboken, New Jersey) can be obtained in all parts of the U.S.A., especially in Italian neighborhoods. Or you can use Westphalian ham from a German delicatessen or in a tin labeled from Holland. Another fine substitute is

Smithfield ham, now available in quarter-pound packages in perfect thin slices.

The classic melon is cantaloupe, but honeydew, Persian, and Casaba melons, and even papaya, are good, too. Generally the melon is sliced into thin wedges with seeds removed and skin cut away, and the meat is served upon the melon.

| Cantaloupe or fresh figs | Prosciutto
Freshly ground black pepper |

Count on 1 small cantaloupe and ¼ pound of prosciutto to serve 4. Or 8 to 12 green figs. Melon needs no preparation other than peeling and may be cut into sections like a flower.

There are a number of ways of serving the combination; place thin slices of ham on top of the melon or arrange the fruit and meat side by side on a platter or on individual plates. Serve with a knife and fork so that each mouthful includes a taste of both, and freshly ground black pepper to taste.
Serves 4.

Autumnal variation: In the fall, when the pears ripen, and later during the winter months, when the russet-skinned varieties are available, serve them with prosciutto. Choose the juiciest pears you can find here. Peel or not depending on the tenderness of the skin; cut into eighths lengthwise, removing the core. Arrange like a flower on the plate, and garnish with strips of prosciutto or salami. A good-quality canned pear that is not mushy could be substituted. Be sure to have plenty of black pepper on hand because the pears seem to need extra seasoning. Even a speck of red, hot, ground chili pepper or a drop of Tabasco would not be amiss.

3
Soups

Pesto

In Genoa, they will tell you that no *pesto* can be authentic unless it is made with their own small-leafed basil and ground in a mortar, not wooden but marble. The basil, moreover, must be grown in a spot where the salty winds of the Mediterranean can blow over it as it matures. They also insist that the cheese must be half Parmesan and half a salty Romano or *percorino*.

However, in this country we are in luck if we can find any variety of garden-fresh basil. The season is short, so when basil *is* in season make a lot of *pesto* and put it in small containers or plastic bags in the freezer.

The principal purpose of *pesto* is for thickening soup, particularly minestrone, but it is also good on fettuccine and even on potatoes.

    4 Tbs. olive oil   4 Tbs. Parmesan cheese (or equal
    2 Tbs. softened butter   parts Parmesan and Romano)
    ½ tsp. salt   4 Tbs. fresh basil leaves
                                6 small cloves garlic

Place in the blender the olive oil, butter, salt, cheese, and basil. Blend 1 or 2 minutes in the blender. Add the garlic; put through the press. (You could, of course, put the garlic into the blender with the other ingredients, in which case you would need only 3 or 4 cloves. But I am always afraid that so much garlic might leave a taste on the blades, whereas the press is easy and seems to extract a more delicate flavor.)

In Italy, *pesto* is stirred into the soup 5 minutes before the soup is taken from the stove. Perhaps you will find it more dramatic to bring the soup to the table in a chafing dish and add the redolent *pesto* there.

Tips about basil: Theoretically basil is easy to grow, even on the windowsill, but it requires quite a bit of attention in snipping back and bursts into pretty but inedible blossoms. Consequently it is a good idea to pick your basil when it is young and tender, with juicy leaves. This is one herb which does not take kindly to drying, not even freeze-drying. It can be stowed in plastic bags in the freezer without blanching and will retain its flavor even though it turns black as a truffle. The taste is adequate but the look is strange.

For all but the most traditional cooks, the blender has replaced the mortar and pestle in preparing pesto.

St. Joseph's minestra.

A good way to store basil is to keep it in oil. Wash and dry the stalks and leaves and stuff them not too tightly into a screw-top jar. Completely cover with olive or any good salad oil and screw the lid on tight. The oil will gradually pick up some of the flavor of the basil, which is all to the good, but be sure to replace with fresh oil so that the leaves always remain completely covered and the jar stays full. Otherwise the basil will spoil.

St. Joseph's Minestra

This soup is served in Italy especially on St. Joseph's Day, March 19, but it is so good that it is often repeated throughout the year.

1 clove garlic
1 large can minestrone
1 can condensed consommé
1 package frozen leaf spinach
Romano or Parmesan cheese, freshly grated
Small bowl of Italian parsley

Rub a saucepan with a cut clove of garlic, just as you would rub a salad bowl. Pour the minestrone into a saucepan, adding water if the directions on the can call for it. Also add the condensed consommé and 1 soup can of water. Bring to a boil. Add the spinach and cook until it is just beginning to soften but still retains its character.

Sprinkle with freshly grated (or freshly opened) Romano or Parmesan cheese. Have a small bowl of chopped parsley on hand, preferably the broad-leafed Italian parsley.

Serve with plenty of crusty bread or brown and serve club rolls.

Serves 6 as a soup, and 3 or 4 as a main supper dish.

Minestrone from Genoa

This great soup from Genoa is often a great surprise to people who think they know a minestrone when they taste it. It has a wonderful lightness and delicacy and makes mere cabbage taste ambrosial.

½ small Savoy cabbage
4 small potatoes
4 small zucchini
4 Tbs. small peas, shelled
1 package quick-frozen green beans (not French style)
1 large can cooked white beans (or 2 or 3 cups cooked dried white beans)
2 stalks celery

16   Italian Cooking

Shred the cabbage. Any cabbage will do but the green cabbage that we call Savoy is quite superior. Pare and dice the potatoes and dice the zucchini, unpeeled. Combine the peas, green beans, white beans, and celery with the cabbage, potatoes, zucchini, and 2 quarts of water. Bring all of this to a boil and simmer gently for about 1 hour.

Serve with grated cheese.
Serves 8.

Lemon and Egg Brodetto

If anyone doubts the close kinship between Greek and Italian cookery, they have only to compare the *avgolemono* soup of Greece with a *brodetto* or broth sometimes called Roman style. For here we have exactly the same combination of lemon and eggs thickening a broth. In Rome, where the Greek influence is strongest, you are likely to have lamb broth. In other parts of the country, it is chicken broth. From time immemorial this soup has taken some slight skill in the making, for the lemon and eggs tend to curdle unless treated exactly right. With a blender, however, there is no problem. The hot broth is poured over the blended egg yolks. In Italy, more often than in Greece, the *brodetto* is made heartier by the addition of toasted bread, in the style of French onion soup. As might be expected, there is usually a sprinkle of Parmesan.

6 egg yolks	6 tsp. grated Parmesan cheese
1 Tbs. lemon juice	
1½ quarts well-seasoned lamb, chicken, or beef broth	12 thin slices Italian bread, toasted

Whir the egg yolks in blender for 1 minute, gradually adding the lemon juice. Have the broth ready in a saucepan, boiling hot. Pour about 3 cups of the broth slowly into the blender while it is still whirring. Then turn the mixture into the rest of the broth and stir with a whisk. Keep hot over a very low burner, continuing to stir until slightly thickened—which should be within moments. Under no circumstances allow it to boil, or you will have scrambled eggs.

Place 2 thin slices toasted crusty bread in each soup dish. Pour on *brodetto*. Sprinkle each portion with 1 teaspoon grated Parmesan cheese. Serve immediately.
Serves 6.

Burrida
Fish Stew

Every region has its own fish stew, or *burrida*, using the local fishes. Most of them begin by cutting off the fish heads, skinning and boning the fish, and producing a broth—a process not too appealing to the average American cook. But this *burrida* can be made from pieces or even frozen fillets of almost any fish, including haddock, mullet, or perch. It makes use of a bottle of clam broth, requires no skinning or boning, and goes together in a flash.

2 lbs. fresh fish (your choice) or frozen fish fillets	2 Tbs. tomato sauce
	1 bottle clam broth (2 cups)
1 medium onion, sliced	½ lb. linguine or other thin spaghetti, broken into short pieces
1 stalk celery, diced	
1 bay leaf	
1 tsp. salt	1 tsp. anchovy paste
2 Tbs. olive oil	3 Tbs. Italian parsley, chopped
1 clove garlic, crushed	

Cut the fish into serving pieces. If frozen, thaw only enough to separate. Place in soup kettle along with the onion, celery, bay leaf (broken in half), salt, and 2 quarts of water. Cook gently for about 20 minutes. This is your base.

A few minutes before dinner, bring back to a boil and add olive oil, garlic, tomato sauce, clam broth, and linguini. Cook about 10 minutes or until linguini is a little softer than *al dente*.

Before serving, stir in 1 teaspoon anchovy paste—a little more or less to suit your taste—and sprinkle generously with chopped parsley.
Serves 4.

Zuppa Alla Pavese

Named for Pavia, a town in Lombardy, *pavese* is the answer when your appetite needs tempting, when you're tired, or when you're hungry and can't think of a thing you want to eat.

4 slices crisp French or Italian bread	1 quart chicken broth or beef bouillon
4 Tbs. butter	4 eggs
	4 Tbs. grated Parmesan cheese

Zuppa alla Pavese.

First toast and butter the bread, or better still, brown it in butter. The bread should be gilded on both sides. Have the broth or bouillon ready, boiling hot. (The richer the broth the better the *zuppa*.)

When serving, place a slice of bread in each soup plate. Break an egg on top of the bread and sprinkle it with one tablespoon grated Parmesan cheese. Pour 1 cup boiling broth into each dish (the heat of the broth cooks the egg just right). Of course, you may use 2 slices of bread and 2 eggs per portion, as is usually done in Italy. Together with a salad and a bit of dessert, this makes as fine a lunch or supper as anyone could wish. Nutritionally perfect, too.
Serves 4.

Stracciatella
Little Rag Soup

In the most sophisticated restaurants in Rome or in a modest trattoria you will find *stracciatella* soup—a broth of a soup with delicate shreds of egg. It is not unlike the Chinese egg drop soup or the *warfel* of Vienna except that it has more body and richness, probably because of the cheese.

Traditional Italian directions say that you must beat eggs together with semolina and cheese for at least 5 minutes with a silver fork; but 30 seconds in the blender will suffice.

1 quart rich broth	2 Tbs. grated Parmesan or Romano cheese
3 eggs	
1 Tbs. cream of wheat or cream of rice	

Bring the broth to the boiling point. Meanwhile place in the blender the eggs, cream of wheat or cream of rice, and grated cheese. Blend; add the mixture to the hot broth slowly, stirring constantly. The egg will cook and break up in delicate shreds. Continue stirring while you let the soup simmer for 3 or 4 minutes.

Grated cheese is usually served with this soup.
Serves 4 generously.

A typical Italian soup tureen.

18 Italian Cooking

Zucchini Soup

Now that good, crisp zucchini is available in a frozen state, this one-time summer specialty can be enjoyed all year round.

1 Tbs. lard or butter	4 eggs, lightly beaten
2 tsp. olive oil	1 Tbs. chopped parsley
6 medium-size zucchini	6 Tbs. grated Parmesan cheese
½ tsp. salt	½ tsp. chopped basil
½ tsp. pepper	

Melt lard or butter in a soup kettle. Add olive oil. When hot toss in the zucchini. Sprinkle with ½ teaspoon each salt and pepper. Stir-fry for 2 or 3 minutes. Add 1½ quarts of hot water. Bring to a boil and cook about 10 minutes. The zucchini will have gone limp but that is as it should be. Meanwhile lightly whir in blender the eggs, cheese, parsley, and basil. With the blender still whirring, pour 2 cups of the boiling hot broth of the soup into the egg mixture and whir 1 minute. Then slowly stir everything together.

Let stand in a warm place, but not over the heat, for about 3 minutes before serving. Serves 6.

4
Seafood

Green Sauce from Bologna
This excellent sauce is most often served with fish or in summer with various types of cold meats. You can make it with a beater but it is much simpler to do in the blender. Instead of the boiled potato you can use leftover mashed potatoes or make up a small amount of instant mashed potatoes from a package.

¼ cup olive oil	1 good-sized boiled potato or about ½ cup mashed potato
3 or 4 anchovy fillets, cut into pieces	1 clove garlic
2 Tbs. chopped parsley	½ small onion, cut into pieces
2 Tbs. capers	2 Tbs. vinegar
6 or 8 small sour pickles	

In a blender or in a bowl, place olive oil, anchovies, parsley, capers, pickles, potato, garlic, and onion. Blend for about 1 minute, being careful not to destroy the identity of the bits and pieces. If, however, you use a beater, you must chop the anchovies, parsley, pickles, and onion and put the garlic through a press. Beat for 5 minutes. While still beating—or blending—add the vinegar and beat a few seconds longer.

Serve in a chilled bowl with broiled or fried fish or sliced cold meats. Especially good with beef or tongue. This keeps very well. You can keep it as you would mayonnaise, well-covered in a jar in the refrigerator.
Makes about 2½ cups.

Barbecued Butterfish
The Italians are almost as adept as the Japanese at frying foods so that they are no more than veiled in crust and devoid of any trace of grease. Their *fritto misto* and assorted fruits of the sea, *frutti di mare*, are exquisite examples of this art. Less heralded, perhaps, is their ability to grill fish or meat and keep it from drying out. This recipe can be used for butterfish, porgies, or any other small, flat fish.

6 small, flat fish	Salt and pepper to taste
1 Tbs. lemon juice	
4 Tbs. olive oil	6 lemon sections (or lime sections)
	Chopped parsley

Clean, wash, and dry fish well. Place fish in a china or glass dish and cover with a bland French dressing made of the lemon juice, olive oil, and salt and pepper. Cover and let stand at room temperature for about 1 hour. Grill over charcoal or an electric broiler for about 10 minutes on each side, brushing occasionally with the dressing.

Serve with lemon sections and a little snipped parsley.

Serves 6.

Italian Fish Fingers

This fish stick recipe is a frank adaptation of one that I tasted in Apulia.

6 Tbs. butter or margarine	2 Tbs. flour
¼ cup olive oil	1 bouillon cube, dissolved in 1 cup hot water
1 large onion, cut in rings	
1 clove garlic, cut in half	¼ tsp. oregano
	½ tsp. salt
	¼ tsp. pepper
2 4-oz. jars sliced mushrooms	2 packages frozen breaded fish sticks
½ cup celery, chopped	Parsley for garnish

Combine butter or margarine and olive oil in skillet. Add the onion, garlic, mushrooms, and celery. Sauté for about 7 minutes or until almost tender. Sprinkle in the flour and mix. Add bouillon, oregano, salt, and pepper and mix well. Cook over low heat for 5 minutes, stirring occasionally. Remove the garlic. Cover the bottom of an ovenproof dish with the mixture. Arrange the frozen fish sticks on top and bake, uncovered, at 450°F. for 12 to 15 minutes.

Serve on a hot platter and garnish with parsley.

Serves 6.

Green sauce for fish.

Skewers of Fish

A most unusual barbecue specialty uses fish instead of meat. The original recipe calls for fresh tuna fish but swordfish or salmon may be used and frozen fish steaks are fine.

3 lbs. fish steaks	Fresh sage leaves
Lemon juice	½ cup melted butter
1 loaf long Italian bread	Salt and pepper
	¼ cup olive oil
Bay leaves	6 lemon sections

Soak the fish steaks in about 1 inch of water with ice and a bit of lemon juice for one hour. Dry on paper towels and cut into 2-inch strips. Cut a long loaf of Italian bread into thin slices. Place on a skewer first a slice of fish then a small bay leaf; next a slice of bread and a fresh sage leaf; and repeat until all the fish is used. You will probably need 6 skewers for this recipe.

Brush fish liberally with melted butter. Sprinkle with salt and pepper and place under the broiler or rather high above the charcoal.

Cook slowly, turning often, and brush with olive oil each time you turn. Don't hurry. The cooking should take about half an hour.

Serve straight from the broiler with lemon sections, which should be squeezed over the skewered fish.

Serves 6.

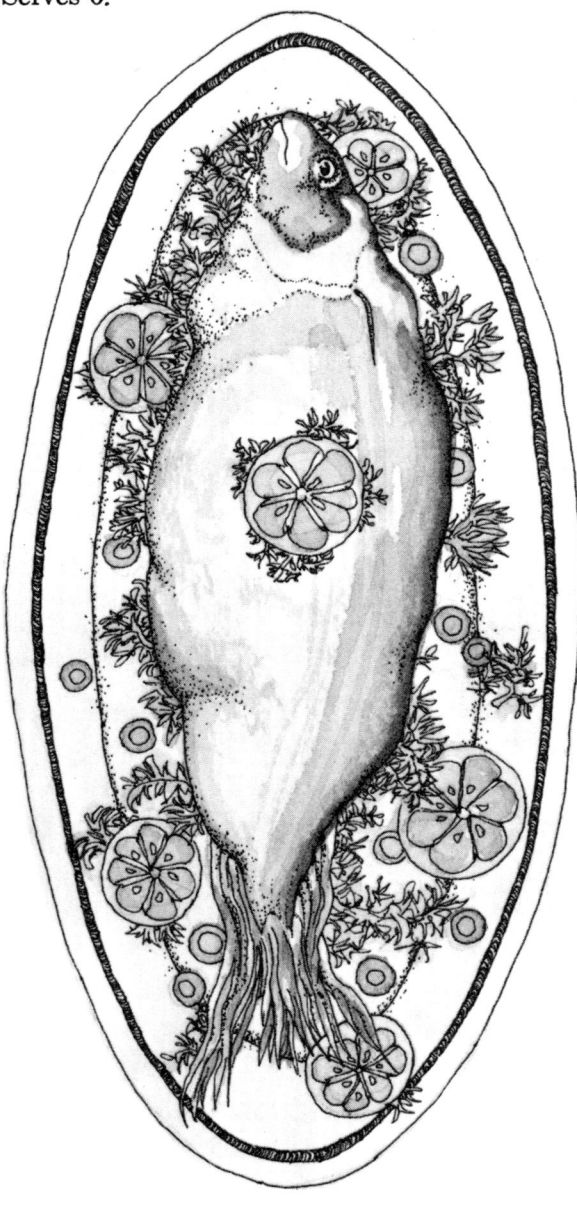

Lobster Alla Diavolo

Much easier to handle than whole fresh lobster, lobster tails are meaty and inexpensive, and they can be prepared and served exactly like whole live lobsters.

The classic sauce for lobsters in Italy is *diavolo*. It is a piquant sauce and excellent, too, with grilled shrimp.

6 lobster tails	½ tsp. pepper
Olive oil (and/or butter) for brushing lobsters	Dash of cayenne or few drops of Tabasco
1 cup canned tomato sauce	½ Tbs. prepared mustard
4 Tbs. vinegar	Parsley, watercress, or lemon sections for garnish
1 cube beef bouillon, dissolved in a little water	

With scissors, cut the lobster tails open on the soft underside. Brush the tails fore and aft with olive oil and/or butter. Place in a shallow pan and bake for 15 minutes in a hot oven (450°F.). While they are baking make the *diavolo* sauce:

In a saucepan, combine the tomato sauce, vinegar, bouillon, pepper, cayenne or Tabasco, and mustard. Mix well and simmer for about 10 minutes.

Serve the baked lobsters on individual plates. Pour sauce over and around lobster and garnish with parsley, watercress, or lemon sections.

Serves 6.

Perch with Clam Sauce

This recipe has been adapted for frozen perch fillets. In Italy, however, it is used all along the coast—especially in the northern regions—with all sorts of saltwater fish. The whole fish, complete with head and tail, appears at the table.

3 lbs. fresh or frozen perch fillets (or other saltwater fish)	2 Tbs. margarine
	2 Tbs. flour
	1 egg yolk
Butter	1 small can minced clams
1 bottle clam juice	
1 onion, minced	1 Tbs. fresh or dried parsley
1 small clove garlic, crushed	White pepper to taste
1 curl of lemon peel	Salt, if necessary

Place fresh fish (or, if frozen, thawed just enough to separate) in a buttered baking dish.

Add clam juice to cover, onion, garlic, and lemon peel. Cover tightly with lid or aluminum foil. Poach in the oven; i.e., bake at 375°F. until fish flakes easily with fork, about 20 minutes.

Meanwhile, melt margarine and stir in the flour. Take fillets from oven and drain. Keep warm while you blend the fish liquor into the flour–butter roux. Simmer sauce until thick, stirring constantly. Whisk an egg yolk lightly and add a little of the sauce to the egg. Then stir the egg into the sauce. (This little trick prevents curdling.) Whisk over low heat a minute or two until the sauce thickens. Remove from fire after the first bubble. Add minced clams, parsley, white pepper to taste, and a little salt if necessary.

Serve, with clam sauce, from the dish in which it was baked. Garnish with parsley or watercress.
Serves 4.

Venetian Scampi Alla Griglia

What are scampi? Ask the question and the arguments are sure to start . . . and rage on and on. On restaurant menus in the U.S.A., the word usually refers to giant-sized shrimp. But in Venice, I was assured that we are wrong. There is, I was told, only one scampi. It comes only from the Adriatic Sea and can be compared with no other seafood in the whole world.

They did consent, however, to impart to me the secrets of preparing scampi.

This is the true and authentic Venetian manner: *alla griglia*, on the grill.

| 2 lbs. jumbo shrimp | Olive oil for basting |
| Salt and pepper | Parsley for garnish |

Cut shrimp lengthwise without removing the shells. Leave one section on the outside joined. Flatten them out like butterflies. Skewer each crosswise with a wooden toothpick to hold it flat. Baste with olive oil; season with salt and pepper. Grill under a hot broiler or on charcoal—first the cut side, then the shell side. This will take 6 to 8 minutes, depending on the size.

Serve on a very hot dish sprinkled with chopped parsley.
Serves 4.

Scampi from the Adriatic.

Scampi Alla Romana

2 cloves garlic	1 Tbs. chopped
¼ lb. shallots or	parsley
onions	24 jumbo shrimp or 36
½ lb. butter	medium-sized
1 Tbs. Worcester-	(fresh or frozen)
shire sauce	1 glass dry white
½ tsp. Tabasco sauce	wine

Chop the garlic and shallots or onions very, very fine and mix with softened butter. Add Worcestershire sauce, Tabasco, and chopped parsley. Mix thoroughly.

Place shrimp on heatproof platter, leaving tails on, and spread over them some of the butter mixture. Cook under broiler for about 10 minutes, turning occasionally. When nearly done, add more of the butter mixture and return to broiler for 5 more minutes. When done, add the remaining butter mixture and leave under the broiler for a few minutes with the flame turned off.

Remove from broiler, add a glass of dry white table wine, and serve immediately with crusty bread.
Serves 6.

Baked Seafood Vesuvio

As a first course or a supper dish to impress your guests, we have devised this version of a popular dish that is usually made of the local crayfish but works very well with good-size lobster tails, especially those from Denmark, which tend to be less dry than some of the others. We have also learned a small trick of pouring a half-inch of clam broth or even hot water into the bottom of a flame-proof baking dish.

4 lobster tails
12 large shrimp, unshelled
12 sea scallops
12 clams in the shell (optional)
½ cup (about) clam juice
4 Tbs. fine bread crumbs
4 Tbs. parsley, preferably Italian
4 Tbs. Parmesan cheese
¼ tsp. dried oregano or marjoram
Salt and pepper
4 tsp. (about) olive oil

Split the lobster tails, as if for broiling (a pair of scissors does a good job), and arrange on a flame-proof dish. Surround with a dozen large shrimp in their shells, sea scallops cut in half, and the clams in their shells. (Clams may be omitted if they are too much trouble.) Pour clam juice over all. Combine bread crumbs, chopped parsley, Parmesan cheese, and oregano or marjoram. Sprinkle with salt and pepper. Dribble with olive oil and set in a moderately hot oven for about 15 minutes, or until the seafood has lost its translucent look, is snowy white, and comes up readily when touched with a fork. The clams—if used—should have steamed themselves open. The liquid in the bottom of the dish will be just about gone.

If the baking dish is attractive, bring it to the table unadorned. If not, mask it in foil. Or if you prefer, you can transfer the whole creation to a heated platter. Be sure to serve plenty of crusty Italian bread.
Serves 4.

Broiled Fillets of Sole Basilica

In ancient Persia, Greece, and Rome sweet basil was a treasured herb. In certain areas of Italy the tradition still exists that a lad is certain to love a lass from whose hand he accepts a sprig of the plant.

Sweet basil is used to flavor and garnish broiled fillets of sole, flounder, or sand dabs of San Francisco—fresh caught or fresh snared from the depths of the frozen food bins!

2½ to 3 lbs. sole fillets
Salt and pepper
4 Tbs. butter, melted
3 Tbs. lime juice
1 tsp. fresh basil (or ½ tsp. dried), chopped
Fresh basil or Italian parsley
Paprika for garnish

Sprinkle the fillets of fish lightly with salt and pepper. Place the fish on a well-oiled broiler rack, lined with aluminum foil for easy cleaning. Brush with a mixture of the melted butter and lime juice. Sprinkle with fresh basil chopped or dried basil that has been soaked for 5 minutes in warm water.

Place in preheated broiler 4 inches away from the heat. Broil for 6 to 9 minutes or until the fish loses its translucent appearance, looks snowy white, and flakes easily when touched with a fork. Do not turn. Do not overcook.

Garnish with sprays of fresh basil, if available, or parsley, preferably Italian parsley. Give to each fillet a ruddy dash of paprika. Serve immediately.
Serves 6.

Fishing boats in the Palermo harbor.

5
Meats and Poultry

Neapolitan Ragout

In little restaurants, as in almost any home in Naples, whether rich or poor, you will find the Sunday ragout. Occasionally, it takes the form of a king of pot roast, where a round of beef is larded with bacon or salt pork. But usually it is a stew made with cubed meat.

3 lbs. round of beef (or 3 lbs. stew meat, cut into 1-inch cubes)	1 Tbs. chopped parsley
2 slices bacon, cut into small pieces	1 large onion, thinly sliced
2 cloves garlic, cut into very thin slivers	1 carrot, thinly sliced
	2 celery stalks, sliced
1 tsp. fresh marjoram	½ cup red wine
Salt and pepper	1 16-oz. can tomatoes
2 Tbs. olive oil	1 small can tomato paste
2 Tbs. butter	2 or 3 bay leaves

Make little cuts in the roast—if using stew meat, make one in each piece. Place in each cut a small piece of bacon, a sliver of garlic, and a sprinkle of marjoram. Sprinkle the meat with salt and pepper.

Heat olive oil along with 1 tablespoon of the butter in a large saucepan. Then add chopped parsley, sliced onion, carrot, and celery. Brown these vegetables slowly over a low flame; then add the meat and brown that, too, on all sides. Add wine and continue cooking slowly until the wine is almost gone. Then add the tomatoes and a can of tomato paste that has been stirred up in ¼ cup warm water.

Cover the pan and simmer about 1 hour or longer or until the meat is tender, adding a little more water or heated wine as needed. Five minutes before removing from the fire add another tablespoonful of butter, broken up into little bits. At the same time add 2 or 3 bay leaves.

Slice the meat if it is a pot roast you are using; or spoon the ragout over noodles, rice, or spaghetti.

Serves 6.

Boiled Beef Slices to Serve with Green Sauce

The slices of boiled beef that are used to make *brodo* (beef broth) are carefully sliced and served separately with sauce. In Bologna it is the famous Green Sauce—see page 20.

Making beef broth is not a difficult operation but it does take a couple of hours of watching, skimming, straining, etc. Moreover, you need marrow bones and sponge bones.

We have invented a way to produce boiled beef in about 15 minutes.

1 lb. chuck steak, cut into slices ½ inch thick	1 small onion, cut in half
1 can condensed beef consommé	2 carrots, scraped and quartered

Lay the meat in a shallow dish. Cover with beef consommé diluted according to directions. Add onion and carrots and bring to a boil. Allow to cook for about 15 minutes or until meat is tender but not shreddy.

It is customary first to serve a cup of the clear broth with thin crusts of bread and grated cheese. Then bring on the boiled beef slices and the green sauce. Potatoes rather than pasta or rice are the classic accompaniment.
Serves 2.

Green Sauce from Tuscany

Allied to the pesto of Genoa but much lighter on the garlic is a sauce that comes from Tuscany. The inspired Bolognese cook from whom I learned it spent the better part of a morning getting it together. But she had no blender.

4 Tbs. olive oil	1 medium-size boiled potato, cut into ½-inch cubes
2 Tbs. vinegar	
4 anchovy fillets, slightly cut up	½ small onion, cut into cubes
3 or 4 sprigs parsley (no stems)	½ clove garlic
2 Tbs. capers	Salt and pepper to taste
6 small sour gherkins	

Place in the blender olive oil, vinegar, anchovies, parsley leaves, capers, gherkins, potato, onion, and garlic. Blend for 1 minute. Season to taste with salt if needed and perhaps a dash of pepper. This makes 2½ cups of sauce.

Keep covered in a jar in the refrigerator and you can have it on hand for weeks. A perfect accompaniment for cold fish, meats, chicken, or turkey.
Makes 2½ cups.

Buds of garlic braided on a string.

Tuscan Pickled Beef

In Milan, there has always been Giannino's restaurant, considered by many connoisseurs to be the finest in the world. Throughout its history, one of the specialties has been a pickled sliced beef—an extraordinarily fine summertime standby, which we admit must be made at least 12 hours ahead of time and allowed to mellow in the refrigerator. In most households, this would probably be a weekend treat.

Meats and Poultry

In Italy, boiled beef—the beef left over from making broth—is generally used. Sliced roast beef is even better. The thinner the slice, the more delicate the dish. Buying roast beef slices from the delicatessen at times proves more economical than cooking the beef at home; there's no waste. Be sure to ask for slices twice as thick as for sandwiches. And *know* your deli man!

2 onions (white or red) finely sliced
3 Tbs. olive oil
½ cup red wine vinegar
1 tsp. sugar
2 cloves garlic
1 bay leaf
1 Tbs. Italian parsley, chopped
½ tsp. dried rosemary or 1 tsp. fresh
2 fresh sage leaves or ½ tsp. dried sage
½ tsp. salt
¼ tsp. pepper
1 cup white wine
1 can condensed consommé
6 or 8 slices cold beef

First, prepare the marinade. Sauté sliced onions in olive oil. Add red wine vinegar, sugar, garlic put through the press, crumbled bay leaf, parsley, rosemary (if dried, rub between your fingers), sage, salt, and pepper. Cook this marinade over high heat for about 10 minutes. Add wine, consommé, and ⅔ cup water. Cook 5 minutes longer.

Meanwhile, place the cold beef slices in a shallow dish. Pour marinade, while hot, over the beef. Cover. Let stand in the refrigerator for at least 12 hours.

The classic garnish includes pickles, olives, pickled peppers and mushrooms, and artichoke hearts in oil. Be sure to provide a pepper mill, a small vial of olive oil, plenty of crisp Italian bread, and some celery or *finocchio*.
Serves 3.

Florentine Chicken Rosemary

Rosemary is an herb to be treated with some caution for it can be overwhelming. In this chicken recipe, however, only a little is used, and in this country we have it powdered, which adds to its delicacy.

¼ cup olive oil
1 tsp. salt
¼ tsp. fresh ground black pepper
½ tsp. dried (powdered) rosemary
2 cloves garlic
2 broilers, quartered

Combine olive oil with salt, black pepper, rosemary, and crushed garlic. Heat in tiny ramekin for about 1 minute. Cool slightly. Then rub the herbal oil over the broilers, both sides, skin and flesh. Broil slowly, flesh side first, 5 inches below the heat. Turn and broil skin side up until brown and crispy.

Two quarters for each person. Garnish with heated plum tomatoes, cut like a flower with a black olive in the center.
Serves 4.

Capretto
Easter Lamb as in Brescia

On Easter Day in Italy, especially in the province of Brescia, they have a particular way with baby lamb—*capretto alla bresciana*. Always this dish is at its best in springtime.

Although it is known as roasted baby lamb —and roasted it is—the cooking is very swift because the tenderest of lamb is used, cut by the butcher into 2-inch cubes.

4 Tbs. olive oil
4 lbs. lamb from leg, shoulder, or rack, cut into 2-inch cubes
Salt and pepper
¼ lb. salt pork, diced
4 Tbs. butter
1½ cups dry white table wine or vermouth
3 twigs of rosemary (fresh or dried)
2 Tbs. brandy
1 cup condensed consommé

Heat olive oil until very hot (375°F.). Sprinkle cubed meat with salt and pepper and sauté on all sides until nicely colored. Meanwhile in a wide, shallow baking pan, place diced salt pork and 4 tablespoons of butter. Heat to a sizzle. Add ¾ cup of white wine or vermouth and the rosemary. Heat again, and add the browned meat. Bake uncovered in a moderately hot oven (375°F.) for about 15 minutes or until meat is tender. Remove meat and keep warm.

Place the baking pan over high heat and let all the liquid boil away, leaving only the rich, brown particles and the fat. Add another ¾ cup of white wine or vermouth and 2 tablespoons of brandy. Cook for 1 minute. Add the condensed consommé, and cook hard for 3 minutes. Make sure to remove with a wooden spoon all the crust or element made during baking from along the sides of the pan. This is the best part of the sauce. If you wish you may further enrich the sauce by adding, a little at a time, 2 to 4 more tablespoons of butter.

Reheat the lamb in the sauce but do not allow to boil hard. The *capretto*, together with the rich sauce is served over *polenta* in Brescia (see page 68).
Serves 6.

Lamb Chops Roman

The Roman way with lamb chops is a method particularly suited to the large, meaty, and much less expensive chops cut from the shoulder. The seasonings are the same as those used in the preparation of the famous *abbacchio* or leg of lamb: olive oil, garlic, rosemary, anchovy, and red wine vinegar.

1 Tbs. olive oil
4 good-size shoulder lamb chops
½ tsp. salt
½ tsp. black pepper, freshly ground
1 small garlic clove, crushed
½ tsp. powdered rosemary
¼ cup wine vinegar
1 anchovy fillet, chopped
Parsley for garnish

Heat olive oil in a heavy skillet. Brown the lamb chops well on all sides over high heat. Sprinkle with salt, freshly ground black pepper, crushed garlic, rosemary. Continue browning for 5 minutes. Add vinegar and hot water, and chopped anchovy. Cover. Cook slowly about 5 minutes longer or until meat is tender.

Garnish with parsley.
Serves 4.

Fegato Veneziano
Liver in the Italian Style

When calves' liver is too expensive, beef liver may be substituted for it in this recipe because the liver is cut into thin strips and will not be tough to chew. Any liver keeps well in the freezer—but not at all in the refrigerator.

Essentially, this is a dish made by the stir-fry Oriental method, with Chinese overtones and souvenirs of the great cuisine of Bologna.

1 lb. calves' or beef liver, sliced about ¼-inch thick
2 good-size onions (red or white), sliced
2 Tbs. olive or salad oil
1 Tbs. butter
½ cup red wine
Salt and pepper to taste
Parsley, finely chopped

Cut frozen or half-frozen liver with a serrated knife into strips about 2 inches long. Cook sliced onions gently in olive oil and butter until soft and golden but not brown; adding a little water to the onions will make them tender and prevent premature browning. Add the liver and heat just until the red color completely disappears. Use a fork, not a spoon. Add red wine and salt and pepper. Bring just to a boil.

Meats and Poultry

Sprinkle generously with finely chopped parsley. Serve immediately with rice, fine noodles, or *polenta*.

Serves 4.

The Pros and Hazards of Deep-fat Frying

Centuries ago, the Orientals, whom the Italians imitate in many ways, turned to the fryer, skillet, and deep-fry kettle as a means of saving fuel and time.

In the past, skill was needed to produce a crisp, dry, nongreasy product. We have developed ways of using the oven in many cases instead of the skillet or fryer; but authentic Italian cookery cannot be divorced from the skillet. The thermostatically controlled electric skillet, which is now generally made deep enough to act as a deep-fat fryer, takes the difficulty out of the whole procedure. You don't have to watch for haze or smoke; you don't have to worry about the chilling of the fat which prevents greasiness; all you have to do is watch the little red eye.

Shallow but deep-fat frying may sound like a contradiction in terms; actually it refers to the use of just enough oil to cover the largest pieces, with at least ½ inch of oil to spare. The skillet should be deep enough to allow 1 or 1½ inches above the oil to prevent spattering.

For this type of frying you may use a shallower skillet instead of one especially designed for deep fat. However, when you have a wider surface and less fat you also have a greater heat loss, and it is a little more difficult to maintain an even temperature. The thermostat sometimes lags. Certain types of dishes like *fritto misto* are well suited to deep-fat frying. It does not work so well for foods that puff in the frying—unless, of course, they are very small pieces.

The thermostatically controlled electric skillet that is deep enough to use as a Dutch oven does an excellent job as a deep-fat fryer. Just be sure that you leave about 1½ inches of space above the oil. Forget all about fry baskets, which are useless.

Always remember that the best results are obtained when you fry small amounts at a time.

In either shallow, deep-fat or regular, deep-fat frying it is good policy to wait five minutes after the little red light of the thermostat has gone off before putting the food into the hot oil. In this way you can be sure that the whole quantity of oil has achieved the desired temperature.

The old-fashioned Italian cook over the centuries inherited the ability to judge the right frying point of olive oil and knew exactly how to combine olive oil with leaf lard (and in northern Italy with butter, too). A great deal of work has been done by scientists concerning the smoking point of oils—a danger signal in terms of health as well as flavor. The arguments still continue but for practical purposes it would appear that butter is the least acceptable (i.e., it breaks down first into smoking point), then comes margarine, followed by olive oil, then lard, and solid shortenings. Salad oils —specifically, vegetable, nut, cottonseed, safflower, and soy oils—all have about the same smoke point. Grapeseed oil, which is little known in this country and not too well-known even in Italy except near Provence, has perhaps the lowest of all but it is scarce and expensive.

The best of the salad oils soak into the foods only to a very slight degree, so frying in deep fat can be far less expensive. You can strain bits and pieces out of oil and save the oil from one occasion to another. Keep it in the refrigerator and always add a small amount of fresh oil to that which has already been used. Above all else, make certain that your oil does not develop the slightest trace of rancidity.

Fritto Misto

The similarity of the Italian mixed-fry to the Japanese tempura can scarcely be accidental. Some say the tempura was brought from West to East by Papal missionaries.

The Italian *fritto misto*, like the Japanese tempura, can be anything from onion rings to seafood strips. The Romans have a particularly interesting combination, easily prepared from canned artichoke hearts. The meat of the dish is often liver.

Roman batter for fritto misto: This batter may be used for seafood and almost any kind of quick-frozen and thawed or very lightly cooked vegetables. It should be thin as heavy cream.

2 cups flour, sifted	4 eggs, slightly beaten
1 tsp. salt	1⅓ cups milk
⅛ tsp. cayenne pepper	3 Tbs. butter, melted

Place the flour in a bowl, and make a well in the center. Add salt, cayenne pepper, beaten eggs, milk, and melted butter. Stir with wooden spoon in one direction until batter is smooth. If you're not going to use it immediately, cover well to keep it from getting crusty.

1 lb. liver (preferably calves')	1 16-oz. can artichoke hearts
	½ lb. mushrooms

Cut liver into convenient bite-size pieces or cubes. (In order to do this you may want to set in freezer for a few minutes.) Drain artichoke hearts and wipe mushrooms. You will be using both stems and caps. With a long-handled fork dip pieces of liver first into batter and allow any excess batter to drip away. Fry liver in deep hot oil at 360°F. Keep it warm, uncovered, in the oven at 200°F. while you dip artichoke hearts and mushrooms into the batter. Fry these, a handful at a time, at a hotter temperature, 375°F. All pieces should be golden brown.

Serve as soon as possible but if you must wait, be sure to keep in a warm place, *uncovered*. The fried morsels may be served on skewers—as in the more elegant places in Rome —or on a platter.
Serves 4.

Fillets of Veal Rosemary

For decades, gourmets in this country have been bewailing the quality—or rather, lack of quality—of American veal. In the old days, the colony in New York had a secret farm where colonists bought milk-fed young veal that was almost as white as turkey and available at its best only for a short season in the spring. Recently, however, veal seems to have improved, perhaps due to different feeding and the fact that people are willing to pay higher prices for younger, whiter veal.

In this particular recipe, you will notice that the veal is a little thicker than most scaloppine, more like a veal steak—about a half-inch thick. And unlike many veal recipes in Italy, this one does not call for pounding.

6 fillets or cutlets of veal, cut from the loin if possible, ½-inch thick	4 Tbs. butter
	4 Tbs. consommé or white wine
Salt and pepper	Small sprig fresh rosemary or ½ tsp. dried
Flour for dusting	

Season the veal with salt and pepper and roll it in flour. Heat the butter until it foams and sauté the veal first on one side, then on the other until it has, as the chefs say, taken on a good color. Pour on the hot consommé or white wine and add rosemary. Cover tightly and allow to cook slowly, without boiling, for about 10 minutes or until the meat is beautifully tender.

Broccoli is the perfect accompaniment for this particular dish, along with a sliced tomato salad garnished with pitted, sliced, or quartered green or black olives and a red wine vinegar dressing.
Serves 6.

Saltimbocca
Leap in the Mouth

Several regions, including Rome and Milan, claim as their specialty a veal cutlet preparation with the intriguing name of *saltimbocca*, a dish so good that it fairly leaps off the plate into the mouth.

6 thin veal cutlets (fresh or quick-frozen), 4″ or 5″ in diameter	½ tsp. powdered sage
	6 thin slices prosciutto or cooked ham
1 tsp. salt	4 Tbs. butter
½ tsp. pepper	3 Tbs. white wine or vermouth (optional)
Hot chili pepper (optional)	

Slice cutlets in half crosswise. Sprinkle lightly with 1 teaspoon salt and ½ teaspoon pepper, and a touch of hot chili pepper, if desired. Strew with sage and place a slice of prosciutto on each cutlet. Top with another slice of veal and pin together with a toothpick. Brown on both sides in 3 tablespoons of foaming butter for a few minutes.

Meats and Poultry

Place on a shallow heated serving dish. To the drippings in the pan add wine or vermouth (or even hot water). Scrape up all the good, flavorsome, brown bits and boil up for 1 minute. Pour over meat in serving dish. Add 1 more tablespoon of butter and allow to stand over the heat for a few seconds longer. All this can be done so swiftly that it makes a great dish to perform with flare at the table. Serves 6.

Super Elegant Saltimbocca

In most elegant restaurants and hotels, mild cheese like muenster or mozzarella is placed between the cutlets along with the ham. In season, black truffles are scraped over the meat with a special silver utensil, in full view of the diner. Often mushrooms are used as a garland; these are first chopped, then browned in olive oil with a touch of garlic and parsley for seasoning. In all cases, the edges of this "super veal sandwich" are pressed together with a heavy knife handle to hold the filling inside.

Scaloppine of Veal Alla Marsala

1½ lbs. veal cutlet, sliced thin and pounded
Salt and pepper
1 Tbs. flour
2 Tbs. butter
1 Tbs. olive oil (optional)
½ cup Marsala wine or vermouth
2 Tbs. chicken or beef broth (optional)

Have veal cutlets cut thin and pounded even thinner. Cut pieces into 6-inch squares. Sprinkle lightly with salt and pepper. Flour lightly. In large skillet, melt the butter; if it seems scant, add 1 tablespoon of olive oil. Brown the

Saltimbocca.

veal a few pieces at a time. It should be quite deep golden on both sides but cooked quickly over high heat so that it is not dry. Place all the pieces together back in the skillet. Add wine or vermouth and allow to cook 1 minute longer.

Place on heated serving dish. Add broth (or water) to the pan, scraping up the bits, and pour over the meat. Garnish with greenery, preferably mint.

Like an elaborate lamb cutlet or what we might call a lamb steak, this scaloppine is often served with a Moroccan touch—dates stuffed with salted pistachio nuts.
Serves 4.

Veal Bolognese

The city of Bologna, in fact, the whole province of Tuscany in nothern Italy, has been called the birthplace of modern haute cuisine. For it was from here that Marie de' Medici took to the court of Louis the inspiration and many of the fundamental principles that later produced the greatest cooking of the Western world.

These collops of veal Bolognese have the classic simplicity of the region. To the food scholar it would be obvious that the recipe belongs to the land where the olive oil and butter civilizations meet, for it calls for browning the meat in oil and butter.

The fountain of Neptune in Bologna, the city considered by many the home of fine Italian cuisine.

8 small, thin (3-oz.) veal steaks or cutlets	1 clove garlic, crushed
Salt and pepper	1 8-oz. can tomato sauce
Flour for dusting	
2 Tbs. butter, melted	¼ tsp. dried basil
2 Tbs. olive oil	½ cup grated Parmesan cheese
1 large onion, finely chopped	

Sprinkle veal with salt and pepper. Dust with flour. Lightly grease a very hot frying pan, quickly pan-broil the veal steaks, and reduce the heat to medium. Meanwhile, combine 2 tablespoons of melted butter and 2 tablespoons of olive oil; sauté onion and crushed garlic until lightly brown. Add tomato sauce and dried basil. Simmer for 10 minutes. Add the meat to sauce. Sprinkle with Parmesan cheese. Set under the broiler to melt the cheese.

Serve from the same dish.
Serves 4.

Stuffed Pillows Vitello

12 small slices veal cutlet, thinly sliced	½ cup sherry or Marsala
12 small slices prosciutto or smoked ham, very thin	Salt and pepper to taste
¾ lb. mozzarella cheese, thinly sliced	2 or 3 drops liquid hot pepper sauce (optional)
½ cup plus 1 tsp. butter	Watercress for garnish

Have veal cutlets flattened with a mallet, paper-thin. Place upon each one a slice of prosciutto or smoked ham. Top with mozzarella cheese, cut as thinly as possible. Fold together like an envelope and seal the sides with toothpicks. Melt ½ cup butter in a large frying pan. Brown the pillows until amber-colored, first on one side, then on the other, turning them gently so that the cheese will stay puffy and not collapse. The cooking time is very

Meats and Poultry

brief. Too much cooking makes the cheese stringy.

Remove pillows from skillet to heated dish. Pour Marsala or sherry into the pan, scraping the bottom and sides. Add 1 teaspoon of butter, salt and pepper, and, if described, 2 or 3 drops of liquid hot pepper sauce. Pour over pillows. Garnish with watercress.

Variation: Use thin slices raw turkey breast instead of veal.

Vitello Tonnato
Tunnied Veal

This famous cold dish combines—surprisingly—veal with tuna fish. Like the German sauerbraten the meat is marinated for a couple of days in a flavorous and creamy, spicy sauce, but unlike sauerbraten the veal is marinated after rather than before cooking. Both dishes show the influence of the Middle Ages when meats and fish were often combined, and oil, vinegar, and spices were necessary for preserving food.

2 to 3 lbs. veal, cut from leg and rolled	2 small carrots
	1 stalk celery
2 anchovy fillets, cut into tiny pieces	2 sprigs of parsley
	3 or 4 cloves
½ onion, cut into small pieces	1 tsp. salt
For Marinade:	
Juice 1 lemon (about 3 Tbs.)	4 oz. canned tuna fish
1 tsp. capers	¼ tsp. black pepper, freshly ground
⅓ to ¼ cup olive oil	4 anchovy fillets

Have the butcher prepare for you a roll of veal, like a pot roast, using 2 to 3 pounds from the leg and removing the bone as well as tendons. The roll should be securely tied to hold it in place. Pierce here and there and insert tiny pieces of anchovy fillets. Place in a deep saucepan with one half onion, cut into serving pieces of anchovy fillets. Place in a deep saucepan with the onion, carrots, celery, parsley, cloves, and salt. Cover with boiling water and simmer, covered, until veal is tender, about 1¼ hours.

Drain veal and allow to cool. Place in a bowl and cover with this special dressing, which may be mixed with a fork, but is much easier and better if done in the blender:

Place in the blender the lemon juice, tuna fish, 4 anchovy fillets cut into pieces, the capers, and pepper. Blend until smooth and, with the blender still running, slowly add ⅓ to ¼ cup olive oil, enough to make a sauce as thick as heavy cream.

Cover the bowl and allow the meat to stand in the refrigerator at least overnight and preferably for about 48 hours, turning occasionally.

Slice the veal thin and cover with the dressing. Garnish with a few more capers and a bit of anchovy. Serve as an antipasto. Or with sliced tomatoes, canned pimientos, peppers, as part of a cold buffet. Crusty bread is absolutely necessary and a not-too-delicate wine. Serves 6.

Tunnied Chicken

In American households where veal is not so popular you may follow the lead of Tuscan housewives who often serve cooked chicken in this style. The chicken is simmered in the usual way (generally without anchovies) and then the meat is sliced, covered with the creamy dressing, and allowed to stand in the refrigerator only a few hours, overnight at the most.

Leftover or sliced chicken from the supermarket or delicatessen may be used.

Tunnied Turkey

Leftover turkey or turkey slices from the market would also be good in this dish. The flavor is less pronounced.

Osso Buco
The Hollow Bones of Liguria

In Liguria, one of the best known meat dishes is called *osso buco*, hollow bones.

4 shinbones, shanks of veal, beef marrow bones, or short ribs of beef (about 4 inches long and not too bare of meat)	½ cup dry white wine
	1 can condensed consommé
	1 Tbs. finely chopped parsley (or 1 tsp. dried parsley flakes)
Flour for dredging	½ clove garlic

Butter for browning
¾ tsp. salt
½ tsp. pepper
Peel of ½ lemon
½ tsp. anchovy paste
1 Tbs. butter

Roll the bones in flour. Place in a heavily buttered skillet along with ¾ teaspoon salt and ½ teaspoon pepper. Cook until well browned, turning occasionally. Add white wine. Cook, uncovered, until the wine is gone. Add 1 cup hot water or condensed canned consommé. Cover the skillet and cook for about 1 hour, adding more water only if necessary.

Five minutes before done, add parsley, garlic put through the press, lemon peel, and anchovy paste. Cook 2 minutes more.

It's a good idea to use the cooking utensil for serving. Or you may place the bones on a heated serving dish. In either case add ¼ cup condensed consommé to the pan gravy along with 1 tablespoon butter. Mix well and spoon over the bones. Serve with rice, polenta, or mashed potatoes. To accompany or follow: salad of Italian greens, including dandelions, escarole, chicory, or field salad.

Serves 4.

6
Eggs, Rice, and Cheeses

Frittata
Italian Omelet

To the French-oriented connoisseur, the Italian *frittata* is considered rather like a poor relation of the omelet.

However, when properly concocted, using a light hand, the Italian *frittata* is a real find for the American cook. It does not require the skill or the special equipment of the cult of the French omelet maker. It is served flat, cut into wedges, and in many ways resembles its cousins from the Orient.

The only problem with a *frittata* used to be how to cook the top side. Today, this can be accomplished with the broiler. All you have to do is cook the *frittata* on one side slowly so as to set the eggs without browning. Use a skillet that can be brought to the table. There is no need to be fancy about this. When the eggs are set to your satisfaction, simply hold the *frittata* under the broiler just long enough for the liquid-look to disappear. Do not brown; it changes the taste.

Unlike the omelet, the *frittata* is not cooked at high heat. Nor is it turned over or folded. You will, of course, find some filled and folded omelets especially in the north of Italy where the two cuisines merge.

One other important point. When cooking a *frittata*, use equal parts oil and butter. The oil keeps the butter from burning.

Frittata Maritate
Eggs Married Italian-Style

This frittata is light and delicate as well as hearty. I add to the eggs not only a little warm water but a dash of lemon and a couple of drops of liquid hot pepper sauce.

- 6 large eggs
- 3 or 4 drops lemon juice
- 2 drops liquid hot pepper sauce
- 2 Tbs. butter
- 2 Tbs. salad oil
- 1 large onion, sliced and separated into rings
- 1 cup spinach cooked, drained, and chopped
- ¼ cup mozzarella, diced
- Salt
- Chopped parsley
- Pepper

Lightly beat together the eggs, 6 tablespoons of warm water (not milk, it makes it tough), 3 or 4 drops of lemon juice, and 2 drops of liquid hot pepper sauce.

Meanwhile, in a heavy flame-proof skillet, melt 2 tablespoons each of salad oil and butter. Add onion rings and cook for about 3 minutes, until lightly browned. Add 2 more tablespoons of water to the onions and cook until the water disappears. (This makes the onions tender but not dry and burned.) Add the spinach and mozzarella. Mix lightly, adding the egg mixture. Allow to cook gently over moderate heat for about 5 minutes or until the bottom is set but not browned. This is a much shorter time than most of the old-fashioned cookbooks suggest.)

Meanwhile, preheat the broiler. When the eggs are cooked, hold them about 5 inches under the heat, for just long enough to absorb the liquid. Do not tan.

Sprinkle with salt and freshly ground black pepper, and chopped parsley. Cut into wedges. Be prepared to repeat the performance . . . it's that good.

Makes 6 wedges.

Uova Divorziate
Divorced Eggs

From one of the world's greatest yacht towns, Portofino, comes a dish called Divorced Eggs. It might be amusing to serve it on a Sunday lunch buffet along with *fritatta maritate*. Obviously, this started out as a leftover dish but it has gained considerable *éclat*. Aside from the delicious potatoes of the region, the dish has a special taste because instead of adding sweet cream or butter—as we might do here in America—they use *crème fraîche*, which is not fresh cream but has a slightly sour edge like ricotta.

Two versions of the basic frittata.

6 cups mashed potatoes, well seasoned
½ cup sour cream
3 hard-boiled eggs
3 cups cooked carrots, coarsely mashed and well drained
Salt and black pepper
Chili peppers, chopped chives, and parsley for garnish

Eggs, Rice, and Cheeses

On a round, heated serving dish, make a mound or truncated pyramid of the mashed potatoes into which you have whipped the sour cream. Cover the top of the mound with the crumbled yolks of the hard-boiled eggs.

Around the base of the pyramid, make a border of mashed, cooked carrots mixed with the diced whites of the eggs.

Because of its bland, natural flavors, this dish takes kindly to plenty of pepper. Provide tiny dishes of finely chopped red chili peppers, a pepper grinder, and a small bowl of chopped chives. Arrange bouquets of parsley or other greenery studding the carrot wreath.
Serves. 6.

An attractive way to store eggs.

Baked Eggs Florentine

The spinach in and around Florence has rounder, thicker leaves and practically nothing in the way of fibrous stems. All summer long it has that first springtime taste and is famous throughout the world. "Florentine" has come to have a special meaning in cuisine, always referring to spinach.

1 package frozen leaf spinach
2 Tbs. butter
2 Tbs. flour
Salt and pepper
1 cup milk
3 Tbs. grated cheese
4 eggs

Cook spinach according to package directions. Meanwhile, melt the butter, remove it from heat, and blend in the flour, ½ teaspoon of salt, ¼ teaspoon of pepper. Add milk and grated cheese. Stir in the cooked, drained spinach. Turn into a greased casserole. Make four "nests" in the spinach in the casserole and break an egg into each. Sprinkle with salt and pepper. Cover and bake in moderate oven (350°F.) for 15 minutes or until eggs are firm.

Serve immediately in same casserole.
Serves 4.

Rice with Pine Nuts

This is a version of *risotto*.

1 cup uncooked rice
1½ cups beef broth
1 tsp. curry powder
Salt to taste
2 Tbs. olive oil
4 Tbs. pine nuts (*pignoli*)

Cook rice in 1½ cups each of beef broth and water, adding the curry to the water and salt according to the saltiness of the beef broth. The rice, as for most Italian dishes, should be a little softer than for American tastes and it doesn't matter if it clings together slightly. For this reason we do not add the olive oil to the water but separately heat it and lightly tan the pine nuts. Stir into rice.

Rice is rarely served with chicken, meat, or fish in Italy but there are exceptions. *Risotto milanese* and this rice with pine nuts often accompany *osso buco* or broiled chicken with rosemary.
Serves 6.

Suppli Alla Telefono
Roman Rice Balls with Mozzarella

For lunch or for a supper or even on a buffet table these make extraordinarily good eating.

1 cup uncooked rice
½ cup butter
3 Tbs. grated Parmesan cheese
1 lb. mozzarella cheese
1 egg
1 cup bread crumbs

2 egg yolks
2 Tbs. tomato paste
Salad oil for deep-fat frying
1 cup tomato sauce (optional)

Cook rice in 4 cups boiling, salted water until very tender but not mushy. Drain the rice. Add the butter and Parmesan. Cool a little. Then add the 2 egg yolks and the tomato paste. Mix well. Cut pieces of mozzarella cheese about 1 inch in diameter and form the rice in balls around the cheese. Dip the rice balls into a lightly beaten egg. Roll in bread crumbs and fry in salad oil, deep enough to cover, at 370°F. until golden brown. When done, the balls will bounce on top of the fat. Drain on paper towels.

Serve hot, plain, or with tomato sauce.
Makes about 12 *suppli*. Serves 6.

Risotto Milanese

The true *risotto* as it is served in Milan is different in texture and taste from any other rice dish. The grains are softer somehow, and more clinging, yet not mushy. To make it perfectly you should use rice grown in Italy. Always there must be a gilding of saffron.

As is often the case in the north of Italy, half olive oil and half butter is used. When making *risotto* you should not wash the rice, for it will spatter when put into the hot fat. Most rice nowadays is clean enough to use, although some housewives insist on wiping their rice with a clean cloth.

4 Tbs. butter
2 Tbs. olive oil
1 cup dry rice
1 onion, finely chopped
1 clove garlic, crushed
3½ cups strong chicken broth
½ tsp. (about) saffron
½ cup Parmesan cheese, freshly grated

In a heavy saucepan melt 2 tablespoons of butter with 2 tablespoons of olive oil. When they are hot (about 350°F.), stir in the rice. Allow the rice to take on a pale gold color, stirring with a fork to keep it from burning.

Add the chopped onion and crushed garlic. Cook a few seconds longer. Add 1 cup hot chicken broth. Cover pan tightly. Cook slowly over low heat for 10 to 15 minutes or until liquid is completely absorbed. Add ½ teaspoon of saffron or more, to taste. (Dissolve the saffron in 3 tablespoons of warm water or in white wine, dry vermouth, or sherry.) Add about 2½ cups more of hot chicken broth. Stir the rice just twice with a fork. Cover tightly and cook until the liquid is absorbed.

Add 2 tablespoons of butter and the freshly grated Parmesan cheese. Stir lightly and serve immediately.
Serves 6.

Risotto Milanese with mushrooms: One half-cup sliced, lightly sautéed mushrooms or soaked dried Tuscan mushrooms may be added to the *risotto* when you add chicken stock the second time.

Risotto milanese.

Green Spinach Rice

This, for Italy, is a revolutionary recipe. It tastes completely unlike *risotto*, has a different texture and a different character. It belongs to the north of Italy where they use a rice that is not supposed to stick together. In this case, we have gone one step further and made it from a precooked packaged rice which theoretically needs no cooking whatsoever. We have often found it easier and safer to ignore the package directions.

1 package frozen chopped spinach
2 cups minute rice
1 tsp. salt

Cook spinach according to directions, but only for 1 minute. Add 2 cups of boiling water,

Eggs, Rice, and Cheeses

Green spinach rice.

the rice, and 1 teaspoon of salt. Bring to a boil again, remove from heat, cover, and let stand for about 10 minutes. Fluff with a fork. Serves 4-6.

Sicilian Arancini
Sicilian Rice Balls or Little Oranges

Sicily claims the credit for having originated this dish. The preparation is exactly the same as for the *suppli* of Rome, but the filling is made of meat and mushrooms.

2 Tbs. olive oil	¼ lb. mushrooms, sliced or chopped
¼ lb. chopped beef and ¼ lb. chicken livers (or calves' liver), cut up, OR ½ lb. chopped beef	2 Tbs. tomato paste
	Salt and pepper
	2 drops Tabasco (optional)
1 clove garlic	Rice ball mixture (See page 38)
½ small onion, finely chopped	

Heat the olive oil in a small skillet; brown the beef and liver. Add a clove of garlic, put through a press, and the chopped onion and mushrooms. Cook gently, just until the red color disappears from the meat—1 minute should do it. Add the tomato paste and 1 cup of warm water. Cook for about 10 minutes. Season with salt, pepper, and maybe a drop or two of Tabasco.

Form the mixture into little balls and form the rice around these balls. Proceed as for *suppli* on page 39.

Serve hot with or without tomato sauce. Serves 12.

Cheese

Before one of my early tasting trips to Italy, I had the supreme good fortune of being indoctrinated with some knowledge of the cheeses of Italy by the late André Simon, who was founder and president of the Wine and Food Society. A Frenchman who spent his life in England, he was probably the most knowledgeable gastronomic authority of our time.

I visited him in his apartment in London when he was 93, and from him I learned that, with the exception of France, Italy has a greater variety of cheeses than any other country in the world. In his opinion the blue-veined Gorgonzola could often challenge Roquefort and Stilton. As for Parmesan, he said, "It stands well ahead of all others as the most suitable cheese for grating and using in cooking."

More and more Italian cheeses are being imported into this country and a tremendous number are produced in the United States under the aegis of experts from Italy or Italian families schooled in the ancient arts. As far as we have been able to gather, practically none, however, use any except cow's milk—no buffalo—no ewe's, no goat's.

Nevertheless, the selection is astounding. These are just a few of the most available across the country.

Parmesan

Since Parmesan is probably the most important Italian cheese in most of our lives, let us begin with this gastronomic masterpiece. The breathtaking, hilly land of Parma in the north of Italy has several claims to fame, but Parmesan adds as much to its renown as the masterpieces of Correggio, the noble smoked hams that come from the nearby hill town of Langhirano, and the purple scented violets that Edwardian ladies pinned to their muffs.

Parmesan, or *parmigiano*, was already famous in the fourteenth century. In one of the tales of the *Decameron*, Boccaccio talks of a country where there is a mountain made of grated Parmesan cheese, on which people live who have nothing else to do but make macaroni and ravioli and cook them in capon broth. Obviously grated Parmesan was used then almost as it is today.

By law, a number of areas in Bologna are now permitted to use the name of Parmesan. And there are, in fact, at least eighteen different kinds available in the city of Parma.

Parmesan, like certain wines, improves with age. Of course, the older it gets, the higher the price. Two years is considered a minimum for a good Parmesan. The extra old, at least 4 years, is chosen by connoisseurs. A good, well-aged, if not ancient, Parmesan can be recognized by the fact that it does not become tacky or stringy when cooked.

However, tastes do change, and not only in America but also on the Continent some people find the taste of true Parmesan too vivid and prefer to use a combination of grated Parmesan and what is known as Romano cheese.

The Grate Controversy: No one argues about the fact that a fine old Parmesan grated over pasta or *risotto* or sprinkled over soup at the table is one of the world's top-flight epicurean experiences.

But times and circumstances have changed. Fine Parmesan is not always easy to get. It is expensive. There is considerable waste.

So we have the temerity to suggest that very good results may be obtained by using a good quality of *freshly opened* commercially grated cheese. Look at the label to see what kinds of cheese are in the jar or package. One of the drawbacks has been the fact that the cheeses were grated too fine. Recently it has become possible to find more coarsely grated cheese.

But here is the important point that cannot be emphasized too much: Make certain that the opened jar or package is airtight. If the cheese comes in a jar, fill the jar with plastic wrap. Keep the cheese (no matter who tells you different) in the freezer or, if you don't have a freezer, use the freezing compartment of your refrigerator. Do not store grated cheese on the side shelves of the refrigerator. The temperature is far too high.

Provolone

Provolone originally denoted the spherical cheeses eaten fresh in the vicinity of Naples.

Now it is made in many parts of the world and it comes in many forms. Sometimes it is shaped like a pear or a melon, a flask, a sausage, a cylinder, a pyramid with its top cut off.

A selection of Italian cheeses.

Eggs, Rice, and Cheeses

plenty of character. Often the *piccante* is made even more distinctive by smoking.

Always look for a smooth, thin, shiny crust, golden-yellow in color. It is a solid cheese, resistant to a dull knife, and should be creamy-white in color. If well made it will have no eyes.

Ricotta

La ricotta is the cottage cheese of Italy. In Escoffier's time it would not have been acceptable unless it were made of the buttermilk of ewes. It owes its special flavor to the fact that it is still made in America as well as in Italy with rennet and is a buttermilky, slightly acid version of cottage cheese. This gives dishes made with ricotta a great deal more distinction than those in which cream cheese has been substituted. It is eaten fresh on bread and served even at the most elegant hotels with sugar and cinnamon, powdered coffee, sometimes cocoa or grated chocolate, and with or without fruit and the addition of a little rum or liquor (see page 74 for *ricotta condita*).

Bel Paese

Bel paese lives up to its name, which means "beautiful country." It is actually a trade name of one of the best known and most popular soft, sweet, mild, quick-ripened Italian table cheeses. Unlike Parmesan, it is of recent origin. There are, however, similar cheeses that have been made for close to a hundred years and sold under various other names, such as Bella Alpino, Bella Milano, Bella Piano Lamobardo, Piemont, Savoia, and Vittoria.

Mozzarella

Next to Parmesan, mozzarella is the most widely known of the Italian cheeses. This is a soft, white, creamy cheese just solid enough to hold its shape. The authorities say that it was originally made from buffalo's milk, but now it is made from cow's milk everywhere. Usually it comes in hand-size ovals, sometimes squares, ranging from a few ounces up to a pound or more.

There is a very small form of mozzarella shaped like an egg and the name naturally is *ovoli*.

Much mozzarella is eaten raw. It is also a

All provolone cheeses, however, have one thing in common—they all show the grooves left by the vegetable fibre cords from which they are suspended as they age.

There are two main types of provolone, *dolce* and *piccante*, sweet and piquant. However, do not be deceived. Even the *dolce* is a cheese with basic component of much Italian cuisine including the inevitable pizza. Occasionally you can buy smoked mozzarella, which is not generally cooked.

Romano

You will not find Romano listed among the classics. The real name is *pecorino romano*. This is one of Rome's most famous cheeses. It, too, was made at one time from the whole milk of ewes. Though it has a hard crust, the texture is somewhat similar to Port Salut. Like Parmesan, it is slightly salty and can be hot and strong-smelling. When fresh it is eaten with bread or biscuits. As is grows older, it becomes a grating cheese and is especially popular in place of Parmesan in central and southern Italy, as well as in America.

Fontina

Fontina is a cheese claimed by both Italy and Switzerland; because it is made not only in Italy but in the part of Switzerland over the frontier. Its full name is Fontina D'Aosta.

Fontina is a fatty cheese with a few holes or eyes like what we call Switzerland's gruyère. It has a smooth texture and is whiter than gruyère, mild and delicate in flavor.

Some people say that the Swiss fontina is better than the Italian for eating out of hand as a table cheese. However, there is no comparison when it comes to using it in a dish of *polenta* because its easy-melting quality leaves a kind of creamy cheese topping as a crown on the golden mush.

Fontina imported into this country during the early autumn often has a slightly smoky flavor (and, incidentally, is most expensive) because it is made not in factories but in the homes of mountain herdsmen. According to reports the cheese is always made from one single milking, so the flavor varies.

It is an experience to watch a crate of fontina being opened in the shop, for each piece needs considerable scraping of the crust before you get down to the cheese. The pieces vary greatly in size and weigh from 4 to as much as 40 pounds.

Gorgonzola

The famous semihard blue-veined, greenish cheese of Italy takes its name from a village near Milan.

The process is elaborate and in many ways similar to Roquefort. The curds are cow's milk, duly salted and matured in cool, damp caves, where it is left in a strong draft. At a certain stage, a red mold sets in and begins to grow over the surface of the curd. From that time onward the cheese is watched, frequently turned, and treated with more care than a newborn babe for no less than three months. It needs another 2 or 3 months, however, to be at its best.

There is a variety of Gorgonzola formerly found only in Italy but now available occasionally in France, Greece, and the United States. It is a white Gorgonzola and has a slightly bitter flavor which brings out lyric poetry among certain connoisseurs, especially when teamed with a fresh pear.

Eggs, Rice, and Cheeses

7
Vegetables

Carrots with Garlic Butter

Italian woodsmen, hunters, and various other roving characters forced to live off their own or somebody else's land developed a number of dishes, including pit cookery, which has since become not only respectable but elegant. *Spaghetti alla carbonara* is one of them and so is this foil-wrapped method of cooking vegetables (they used leaves).

2 cups fresh or frozen carrots, thinly sliced (thawed)	2 Tbs. butter ¼ tsp. salt 2 to 3 cloves garlic, crushed

Add to the carrots the butter, salt, and crushed garlic.

Cook in foil over charcoal for about 20 minutes, or in a 350°F. oven, turning once.

The most interesting way to serve the vegetables is in their wrappings with an "X" cut in the center and the edges folded back.
Serves 4.

Eggplant Marinara from Calabria

Calabria is a cornucopia of glorious vegetables as well as seafood—broccoli, cauliflower, and eggplant in many sizes and colors from white, purple-striped to midnight hue. A delicious antipasto that keeps for weeks in the refrigerator is made this way:

1 large eggplant ½ cup white vinegar 1 tsp. salt ½ tsp. pepper 2 cloves garlic	1 tsp. fresh oregano, chopped, or ½ tsp. dried (or same amount of basil) 1 cup Italian olive oil

Cut the eggplant into half-inch cubes, leaving the skin on. Cover with water and cook uncovered for about 7 minutes. Drain very well. Then place in a large bowl with the vinegar, salt, pepper, garlic cloves put through a press, and oregano or basil. Cover and let stand in the refrigerator overnight.

Add olive oil and mix well but lightly, so as not to break the eggplant cubes. Serve with plenty of crusty bread.
Serves 8 as an appetizer, 4 as a main course.

Piselli con Prosciutto
Infant Peas with Prosciutto

Rome claims credit for this most elegant of all vegetable dishes. But you will find it in many parts of Italy. It requires the most infantile peas, so small that most farmers would consider it a sacrilege as well as an enormous extravagance to pick them. And most cooks would quail at the thought of shelling enough to serve four as in this recipe. A few years ago they were almost unobtainable in this country but now—at a price—you can buy them frozen.

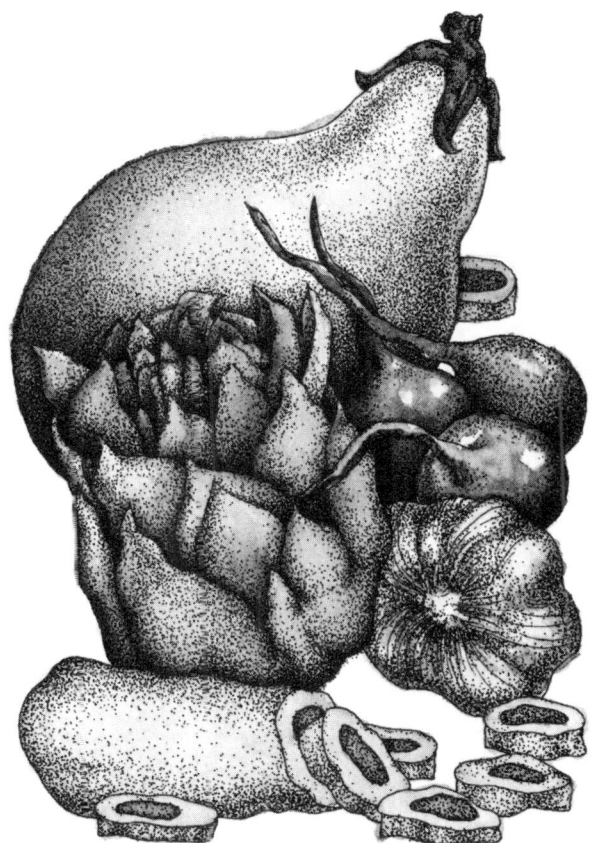

¼ cup butter	½ tsp. salt
1 small onion, thinly sliced	½ tsp. sugar
	¼ tsp. pepper
2 cups shelled baby peas or 1 package frozen	6 thin slices prosciutto

Melt butter in a heavy saucepan and gently brown the onion, adding a spoonful of water if the onion seems to be cooking too fast. Add the peas, ½ teaspoon each of salt and sugar, ¼ teaspoon pepper, and 2 or 3 tablespoons of water. Cook briskly until just tender; all depends on the age and size of the peas you use. Stir frequently with a fork to prevent sticking. Shred the prosciutto finely and add to the peas. Lower the heat and cook a couple of minutes longer to heat the prosciutto.

Some people add a bit of chicken stock to the peas for a soupier vegetable dish. In that case, they are generally served in a dish that looks like one of the old-fashioned bird baths of our grandmothers' time.
Serves 2.

Tuscan Mushrooms on Toast

Florence as well as the towns of Fiesole and Assisi are famous for mushrooms that grow in autumn underneath the chestnut trees. To enjoy them fresh you must go there in October, but any time of the year you can have a number of specialties made of the plump, dried fungi of Tuscany. These, by the way, can be

Piselli con prosciutto.

Vegetables

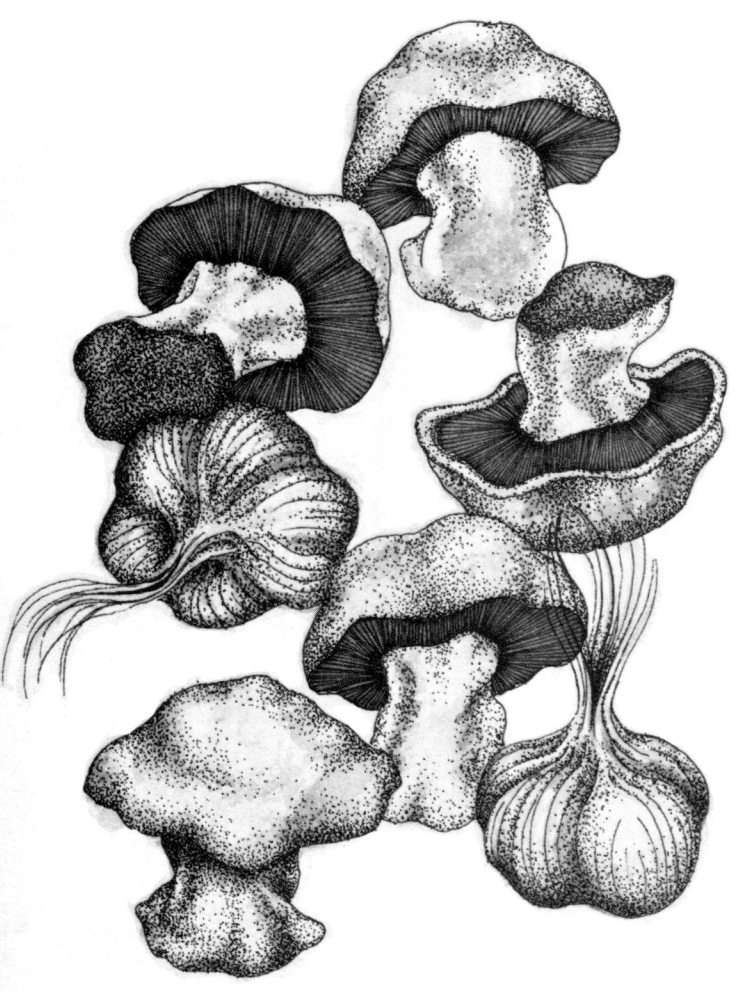

utes. Season with ½ teaspoon salt and ¼ teaspoon white pepper. Add the Chianti and continue cooking uncovered for about 10 minutes longer or until mushrooms are quite tender. Cut the Italian bread into strips and brown on both sides in butter.

Place the cooked mushrooms over the toast and serve garnished with thin strips of Italian prosciutto.
Serves 4.

Crusted New Potatoes Oregano

In northern Italy potatoes are often more popular than pasta or rice. This unusual recipe is particularly well adapted to small, new potatoes or even frozen, small potatoes. The shallow deep-fat frying method described on page 30 may be used.

12 small, new potatoes or frozen, small potatoes	½ cup chopped oregano, parsley, and chives, mixed
4 Tbs. butter, melted	Deep oil for frying

Cook the potatoes in boiling salted water until almost done, slightly resistant to the fork. (If you use frozen potatoes cook them unthawed.) Drain but do not dry. Brush with melted butter and toss in a bag or roll in finely chopped herbs. Almost any combination is good but we like about ⅓ each chopped oregano, chives, and parsley.

Drop a handful at a time in deep oil at 370°F. and cook for about 3 minutes or until the butter and herbs have formed a crust on the potatoes. Drain on paper towels.

This is one dish where cooking and serving should be instantaneous. You may want to proffer coarse kosher salt or seasoned salt and pepper as a garnish.
Serves 4.

Leaf Spinach with Pine Nuts and Raisins

No vegetable dish could be more Italian, yet, like so many others, it shows the influence of the Moors. Escarole, which is cooked in Italy far more than it is here, may be prepared in much the same fashion. In this case

found in many Italian-American markets in the States including Manganaro Foods, Inc., 488 Ninth Avenue, N.Y.C., who will ship all kinds of Italian delicacies to any part of the United States.

¼ lb. dried mushrooms	¼ tsp. white pepper
1 Tbs. butter	½ cup Chianti wine or dry sherry
1 Tbs. olive oil	4 slices Italian bread
½ tsp. salt	Thin strips of prosciutto

Soak the dried mushrooms in warm water to cover, for at least 15 minutes. Drain and press out the water. Cut into small pieces or thin slices and cook in 1 tablespoon of butter and 1 tablespoon of olive oil for about 5 minto save time and effort, we are using leaf spinach, one of the best of the frozen vegetables. After draining, dry the spinach slightly on paper towels. The sweetness of the raisins adds to the garden-fresh, just-picked flavor.

4 Tbs. olive oil
4 Tbs. pine nuts (*pignoli*) or salted pistachio nuts
2 packages frozen leaf spinach, cooked and drained
1 cup seedless raisins
2 cloves garlic, crushed

Heat olive oil in a frying pan; add nuts, cooked and drained spinach, raisins, and crushed garlic. Cook gently for about 5 minutes.

As in France, an extra-special dish like this one is often served in regal grandeur on its own either before or after the meat dish. Serves 6.

Stuffed Tomatoes, Royal Danieli

These stuffed tomatoes are typical of the many delicious rice dishes of Venice. When large, they are often served hot as a luncheon entrée. The smaller tomatoes make a delightful appetizer when chilled.

4 large or 6 medium-size or 8 tiny tomatoes
1 cup uncooked rice
2 cups tomato juice
⅛ tsp. cinnamon
1 Tbs. chopped parsley
½ to 1 clove garlic
¾ tsp. salt
½ tsp. pepper
2 Tbs. butter or olive oil
2 Tbs. olive oil

Cut tops off tomatoes; scoop out seeds; and cut the tomato pulp into small pieces. Cook the rice in the tomato juice with cinnamon, chopped parsley, crushed garlic, ¾ teaspoon of salt, ½ teaspoon of pepper, and 2 tablespoons of butter or olive oil to add richness.

Combine the tomato pulp with the cooked rice. Place the mixture in the tomatoes and sprinkle with 2 tablespoons of olive oil. Cover each tomato with its own top, place in a well oiled or buttered baking dish and bake uncovered at 400°F. for 10 to 12 minutes, or until the tomatoes are well heated and puffy.

The Campo dei Fiori market in Rome.

Vegetables 47

Serve chilled as a first course or hot as a luncheon entrée.
Serves 4.

Zucchini Allumette
Zucchini Straws

In the Piedmont areas in Italy you will be served in summertime a vegetable that looks almost like a crisply gilded spaghetti. Actually it is young zucchini cut into long thin shreds and deep fried in oil but not brown, only ever so slightly gilded. You should provide at least one zucchini for each person.

6 medium-size zucchini	1 cup flour Salad oil for frying Salt and pepper

Wash zucchini. Unless the skins are tough it is not necessary to peel them. Cut by hand or put through a shredding machine so that they are in long, thin strips. Place in a paper or plastic bag along along with about 1 cup of flour. Shake until evenly coated.

Heat salad oil to 375°F. Shake off any excess flour from the zucchini and fry a handful at a time, just about 3 or 4 minutes or until palely gilded. (For deep-fat frying instructions see page 30.)

Serve hot as an appetizer, with cocktails, or as a vegetable.
Serves 6.

8
Pasta

Sensational New Way to Cook Pasta

Forget all you have ever learned about cooking spaghetti—timing, rinsing and so on.

In a large kettle boil up 3 quarts not 6 quarts of water to cook 1 pound of pasta. Add 1 tablespoon of olive oil or salad oil. The oil prevents sticking and guards against boiling over.

When water is frantically boiling, add the pasta. Cook one-half the usual time. Cooking time depends upon type of pasta. Turn off heat. Let stand uncovered in a warm place for at least 10 minutes or until you are ready to serve the pasta. The gradually cooling water provides its own thermostat and automatic cutoff. If pasta should become too cool bring it to a boil and serve immediately.

Any leftover can be kept in the water in the refrigerator to be reheated and served promptly.

Otherwise bring the big (handsome, we hope) kettle to the festive board. With a big strainer, scoop up portions of spaghetti and provide sauce for tossing.

Homemade pastas cook so quickly that they need only to be brought to a boil. Certain others, however, like wagon wheels and large shells, require much longer time to cook and swell.

Cooked in this way, pasta becomes party food.

For parties it is all important to have a way to cook spaghetti so that it never sticks together. And what is equally exciting, it stays late and soon, perfect in texture for early arrivals and late comers. At all times, it is properly cooked so that, as the Italians say, *sempre al dente*—"so that it gives a little work to the teeth."

Homemade Pasta

Although it sounds difficult to the modestly trained cook, it is not an impossible task to make the zenith of Italian glories—homemade pasta. Those who take the task seriously go to the trouble of having imported from Italy a noodle rolling pin carved of a special wood and at least 27 inches long. Last year it was $8; now the price hovers around $10. So even the most

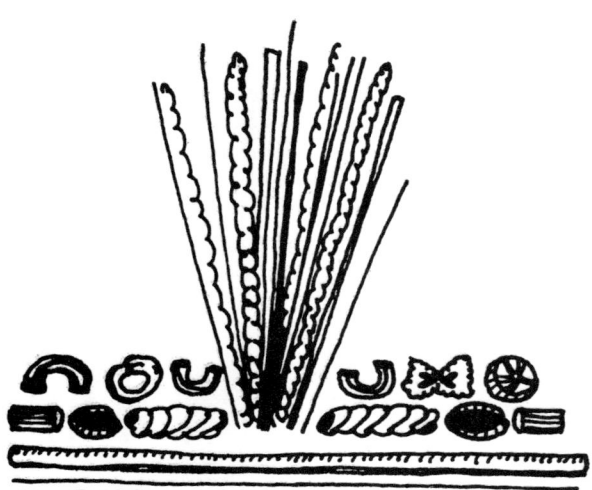

The delightful and varied shapes of pasta.

affluent gourmets are being tempted by noodle-making machines now available in specialty shops and the gourmet sections of department stores. There are some renegades who will tell you to add 1 or 2 tablespoons of warm water to the dough but this practice is frowned upon in most knowing circles. You can argue for hours about the best kind of flour. The best in Italy is considered to be made of hard winter durum wheat. But, in fact, few consumers have access to anything except all-purpose flour, from which you can make a good, though not celestial, pasta of your own.

3 cups sifted flour	1 egg yolk
1 tsp. salt	Small amount of
3 whole eggs	olive oil

In a large bowl place sifted flour mixed with 1 teaspoon salt. Make a depression in the center. Add the eggs and egg yolk, and work together to form a dough that is quite stiff. If necessary, add a little more flour. Form into a ball. Rub the outside with a little olive oil or salad oil and allow to stand, lightly covered, at room temperature for about 3 hours.

Divide into 2 or 3 balls and roll out thin. Fold over and over into a jelly roll form and cut into ¼-inch strips for fettuccine—or make whatever size you like.

If you have a noodle-making pasta machine, follow the package directions, which are now blessedly written in English. The first one we bought in Milan had all the instructions in Italian. After the noodles are cut, unravel and spread out to dry—but do not allow them to become bone dry.

Cook like any other pasta but only half the time.

Serves 6.

Alfredo's Fettuccine

You use equal parts of noodles (preferably homemade), butter, and cheese to make Alfredo's fettuccine. It is very rich, but on the other hand, simple and very good. You should have fresh, unsalted butter and fresh cheese that you grate at the table immediately before using. If you have any grated cheese left over you can keep it in the freezer but not on the shelf or even in the refrigerator.

1 lb. homemade or packaged noodles	½ lb. sweet whipped butter, cut into bits
1 Tbs. olive oil or butter	2 cups Parmesan, freshly grated

Cook the noodles in boiling salted water with olive oil or butter added to the water. You will find that homemade noodles become tender rather more quickly than the bought variety. Do not overcook; the noodles should not be mushy.

Drain. Place in a large, well heated bowl and add the bits of whipped butter and the grated Parmesan cheese. Toss and mix thoroughly. Cream is not necessary.

Dish up without delay and serve with a green salad and slices of ham. Instead of the salad you might have fresh asparagus in season. The asparagus can share the butter and cheese sauce of the pasta.

Serves 4 to 6.

Green fettuccine: Use green (spinach) noodles. These you can buy anywhere.

Anchovy Sauce for Pasta

This dish will leave tears in your eyes if you use too much of the crushed chili peppers. Fresh-ground black peppercorns give somewhat the same taste but are not authentic.

It might be a good idea to serve the red pepper separately in a sprinkler jar. For those who are not partial to anchovies, a small can of sardines may be substituted.

¼ lb. (1 stick) butter
½ cup olive oil
3 or 4 cloves garlic, unpeeled
1 1¾-oz. tin flat anchovy fillets
¼ cup fresh parsley, minced
Grated Parmesan or Romano cheese (optional)
Freshly ground black pepper or crushed red chili peppers (optional)

Heat together the butter and olive oil. Allow to bubble but don't boil.

Smash flat with a cleaver unpeeled garlic cloves (unpeeled because you want to remove them intact before serving). Cut the anchovy fillets into 1-inch pieces and add them, with their oil. Cook gently without browning until anchovies are practically invisible. Add the minced parsley and cook 2 minutes longer. Serve with or without grated cheese, and/or sprinkle with finely crumbled red-hot peppers. Serves 6.

A set of copper measuring cups, which hold different quantities than our own.

Linguine Felice alla Cauliflower

Cauliflower, often a pale mauve color in Italy, is known poetically as "the flower vegetable of the minor gods." Although it would shock the classicists, we use frozen (white) instead of fresh cauliflower. At our market, it costs half as much right now. Besides, the recipe requires cooking until the vegetable is softly tender, so the crispness of fresh cauliflower, its major asset, is lost!

1 lb. linguine (or spaghetti, vermicelli, or noodles)
6 Tbs. leaf lard, butter, or margarine
6 Tbs. salad oil
2 packages frozen cauliflowerets
1 small can plum tomatoes
1 clove garlic, crushed
1 tsp. salt
½ tsp. pepper
¼ cup fresh (or frozen) Italian parsley, snipped
Grated Parmesan or Romano cheese

Prepare linguine according to directions on page 49. We hope you have found some leaf lard. It is inexpensive and exceptionally flavorful. If not, use butter or margarine, and heat together with oil (it need not be olive oil; any good salad oil will do). To bubbling grease, add: frozen cauliflowerets, plum tomatoes with their liquid, crushed garlic, 1 teaspoon of salt, ½ teaspoon of freshly ground black pepper, and snipped parsley. Cook, uncovered, until sauce begins to take on a slightly thickish consistency. Break up tomatoes with fork but do not allow them to become mushy.

Cover linguine generously with grated Parmesan or Romano cheese.
Serves 6.

Pasta alla Vongole Bianca
Pasta with Little Clams in White

All manner of pasta and spaghettis are served in Italy with tiny whole clams or with chopped clams, but there are two entirely different dishes that may be brought to you. In Naples and also in Rome you are likely to find your clams sauced with tomatoes and garlic and oil. But in Venice, they come delicately done up in white with nothing much added except a little butter or oil and butter, and sometimes chopped parsley or a very small amount of mild ham.

3 pints small steaming clams *or* 1 8-oz. can minced clams and 1 8-oz. bottle clam juice
6 Tbs. butter
1 Tbs. lemon juice
1 clove garlic, crushed
¼ tsp. white pepper
¼ lb. lean prosciutto or Westphalian ham, diced, and/or fresh Italian parsley, chopped

Add 3 tablespoons water to 3 pints of small steaming clams. Allow to steam until they open. Take immediately from the heat, remove shells, and strain the juice.

If you are using minced clams and bottled clam juice, simmer the clam juice for a few minutes.

Remove juice from the fire; add the butter bit by bit and stir until it is all melted. Season to taste with lemon juice, crushed garlic (if desired), and white pepper. Return the clams to the sauce. Heat but do not allow to boil.

Have ready the prosciutto or ham and/or small bowlful of chopped parsley.

At the table mix together the ham and the clams, in their lemony-buttery juices. Toss with a fork. Serve on heated plates. In some parts of Italy the various ingredients are passed in separate bowls and each person does his own saucing and mixing.

Serves 6.

A traditional way to form dough for ravioli.

Ravioli Embellished

Those who have had the good fortune to eat in Capri before the days of the tourist invasion or to be entertained in homes where ravioli are handmade, hand-stuffed, and cooked in clear golden broth and unadorned as sunlight will have no part of what we in America have learned to accept as one of our staple quick dishes. But there is no doubt that acceptable ravioli, round as well as square, do come in cans and frozen packages. With a little embellishment they make a good quick lunch or supper.

2 jars or packages ravioli in tomato sauce
2 Tbs. olive oil
1 Tbs. fresh or 1 tsp. dried oregano
½ cup mild grated cheese

Place the ravioli in tomato sauce into a shallow, greased casserole. Dribble with olive oil. Sprinkle with oregano and cover lightly with ½ cup grated cheese (you could use equal parts Romano and Parmesan, provided the Parmesan is not too sharp). Bake at 350°F. for about 20 minutes or until bubbly but not crusted.

Especially good with a watercress or endive and beet salad, crusty bread, and a hearty dessert like baked apples.

Serves 4 as a main dish.

Spaghetti Amatriciana

After years of listening to people talk about the glories of long-cooked tomato sauce for spaghetti, I was delighted to discover in a trattoria near Rome a tomato sauce that tasted as if the tomatoes had been only a few minutes off the vine. For years on and off, I kept sleuthing this sauce, *amatriciana*, until I discovered it in Nika Hazelton's book, *I Cook As I Please*.

She calls it "a specialty of Roman *trattorie*. The sauce is made from pork fat rather than olive oil and quickly cooked so that the tomatoes taste fresh. The traditional cheese used with this sauce is the sharp, pungent *pecorino*." But she recommends either a mixture of Parmesan or Romano or Parmesan alone.

If you can't get fresh tomatoes, a large can of Italian plum tomatoes is a permissible substitution.

½ cup minced fat bacon
2 Tbs. olive oil
4 Tbs. minced onion
1 clove garlic, finely chopped
¼ cup parsley, finely snipped
1½ lbs. ripe plum tomatoes
Salt and pepper
1 lb. cooked pasta, preferably spaghetti
1 to 2 Tbs. butter
1 cup Parmesan cheese, freshly grated

Place the minced fat bacon in a saucepan, cover with cold water; bring to a boil and drain. Combine with olive oil. Add the onion, garlic, and parsley. Cook over medium heat, stirring constantly, for 3 or 4 minutes or until onion is golden. Add the tomatoes, and salt and pepper to taste. Bring to a boil. Lower heat; simmer uncovered for 15 minutes or until the tomatoes are just cooked (if you use canned tomatoes, eliminate the simmering).

When the sauce is to be poured over the cooked pasta, stir in 1 or 2 tablespoons butter. Serve with grated Parmesan.
Serves 4 to 6.

Spaghetti alla Carbonara

The word *carbonara* refers to the men who make charcoal in the forest region of the Abruzzi. In the winter the men took with them bags of spaghetti, smoked hams, olive oil, hard cheese. Fresh eggs could be "liberated" from farms and there was always red or black pepper to be crushed.

Nowadays spaghetti in the *carbonara* manner appears in the most elegant dining places, but the woodsmen's technique is still used. Some elegant chefs use a little cream, but this is heresy.

6 slices raw, smoked, uncooked ham (prosciutto, Westphalian ham, country-smoked pork shoulder, or Canadian bacon)	2 Tbs. olive oil 1 lb. spaghetti 6 eggs Black pepper, coarsely ground, or Java cracked pepper Parmesan cheese, freshly grated

Cut prosciutto or ham into thin strips and cook in olive oil. Cook spaghetti as on page 49.

Provide for each person 1 raw egg and plenty of pepper. Have a bowl of freshly grated Parmesan cheese on hand, too.

Each person breaks the egg onto his portion of spaghetti and mixes it rapidly with the hot spaghetti so that the heat of the pasta actually cooks the egg. Add the ham with olive oil and sprinkles of coarse pepper and grated cheese. Then mix some more.

The mixing of the *carbonara* can be done by the cook in the kitchen but the ritual is far too interesting to be unseen.
Serves 6.

Genoese Spaghetti Sauce

In Genoa and the surrounding countryside, they have a habit of serving their pasta, particularly the fine spaghetti, all aglisten with

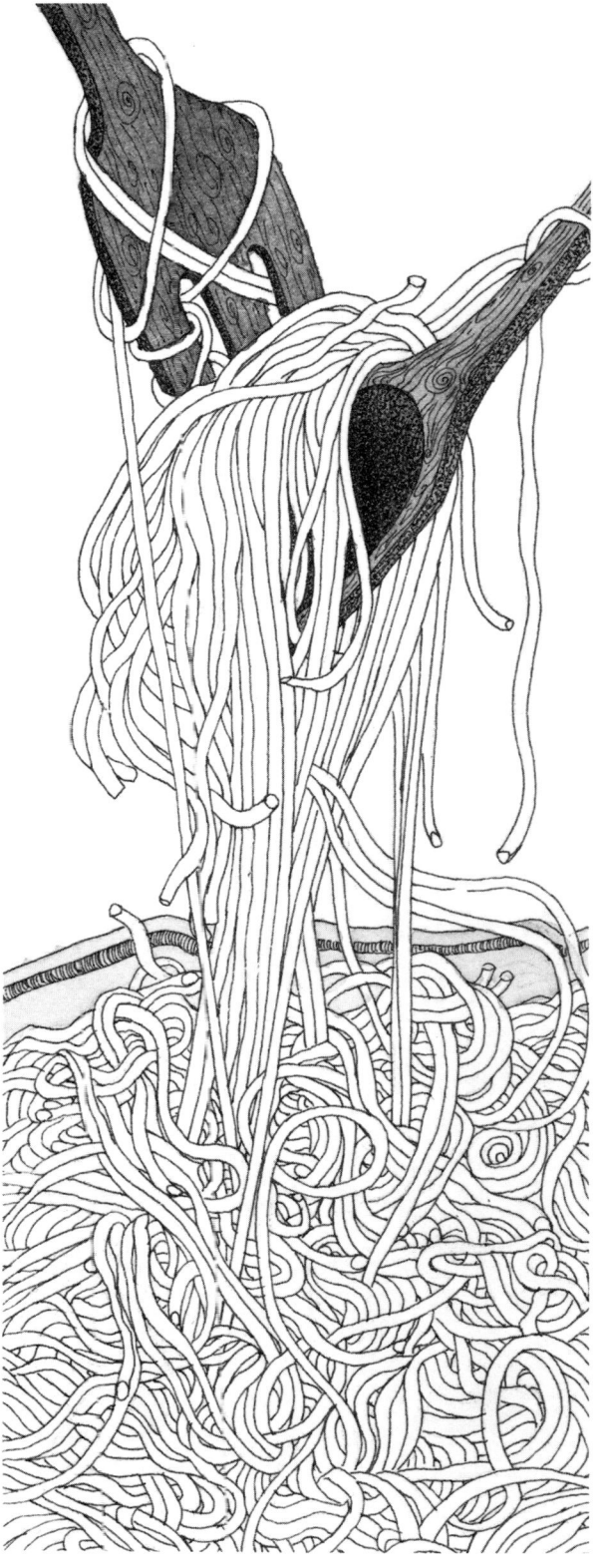

butter and olive oil and flecked with fresh herbs like basil and parsley. Use fresh basil and fresh parsley, if you can get it, but when you can't, it is possible to make the dish by allowing dried herbs to steep, covered, in lukewarm water for half an hour. Drain.

1 good-size onion
4 cloves garlic
¼ lb. butter
4 Tbs. olive oil
12 sprigs fresh basil, chopped
12 sprigs fresh parsley, chopped
½ tsp. salt
⅛ tsp. pepper
Grated Parmesan cheese

Chop the onion finely and put the garlic through the press. Cook both slowly in the butter and olive oil in a frying pan. Cook only until the onion is pale gold.

Add basil and parsley. You should have about ½ cup fresh herbs or about 4 tablespoons dried herbs.

Cook the herbs and onions together for 5 minutes. Add 2 cups of hot water, the salt and the pepper. Simmer uncovered for about 15 minutes.

Serve this sauce in a heated bowl. Each person adds the sauce to his own spaghetti, along with little bits of butter and grated Parmesan cheese, and mixes the sauce into the spaghetti until the strands are glistening.
Serves 4.

Spaghettini with Tuna Sauce

2 Tbs. olive oil
1 Tbs. chopped parsley
½ tsp. dried oregano
1 7-oz. can flaked tuna fish
1 clove garlic, crushed
1 15-oz. can tomato sauce with tomato tidbits
½ tsp. dried basil
1 lb. thin spaghetti or noodles

Lightly brown the tuna fish in olive oil with the garlic and parsley. Add the tomato sauce and cook for 5 minutes. Add oregano and basil. Cook 5 minutes longer. Makes about 1½ cups sauce. Cook the spaghetti or noodles, pour and toss this Sicilian sauce.
Serves 4.

Quadrettini
Four-faced Pasta

Never since I can remember has the San Marino Restaurant on East 53rd Street in New York City given away any of their recipes, particularly the secret of their special pasta dish, *quadrettini*, made of four ingredients.

But we begged so hard and experimented on our own so often, coming so close to the original, that the sons of the founder Antonio Gugnoni, Walter and Fred, took pity on us and relented.

We had not tasted it in Italy but they told us it had been brought by their father from Maldola, a little village near Forli in the vicinity of Bologna.

Though it tastes so unusually delicious, the big secret seems to be fairly simple: cooking broken-up wide noodles in a rich broth.

Spaghetti with Genoese sauce.

1 16-oz. package wide, double XX noodles
2 quarts combined chicken and beef broth (homemade, canned, or from cubes)
1 package frozen chopped spinach
¼ tsp. nutmeg
Salt and pepper to taste
6 very thin slices prosciutto
2 Tbs. butter
1 cup grated Parmesan cheese

The double XX noodles we suggest using for this recipe are particularly rich in eggs and come already broken into pieces about 2 inches long. Break them up into smaller bits. Drop into combined chicken and beef broth and cook 8 minutes. These are not supposed to be *al dente*. While the noodles are cooking, shred the prosciutto and cut into bits; sauté in the butter until heated through but not dry or crisp. Cook the spinach according to package directions. Flavor with nutmeg, and salt and pepper to taste. Drain noodles and spinach and combine. Combine ham with noodles and spinach. Keep warm.

Be sure the mixture is hot. Stir in grated Parmesan cheese and toss until the cheese is completely melted and becomes indiscernible. This dish may be served as a first course in the Italian fashion or as an accompaniment to a meat dish. Makes a fine supper or luncheon ringed with sautéed, browned sausages, Italian or otherwise.

Serves 4–6.

A Galaxy of Pastas

Try as many types of pasta as your local store carries; many of your old favorite dishes will take on a new look when you vary the pasta. The very thin spaghetti (*vermicelli*) twirls beautifully when you hold your fork against a tablespoon. The spinach macaroni ribbons add a springlike note of green. Prettiest of all, perhaps, are the shells, dainty miniatures of the big seashell of your childhood, which, when held to the ear, echoed the sound of the ocean surf.

Vary the type of pasta according to your timetable, too. You can cook very thin spaghetti in 2 to 4 minutes, on the night you want to make the early show. When time is less important, plan to use *rigatoni*, the large, grooved, cut macaroni that takes 16 to 20 minutes to cook. The various sizes, shapes, and types are generally interchangeable in recipes. Here we have given more or less traditional timing, presuming you will consume these dishes immediately. Here are some suggested combinations.

All these quick, handy-for-emergency pasta dishes are designed to serve 2 or 3.

Perciatelli (thin macaroni) with Liver Sauce: Allow about 10 minutes for cooking thin macaroni (*perciatelli*). Blend 1 can liver pâté thoroughly into 1 cup tomato sauce. Put 1 clove garlic and ¼ small onion through garlic press, add to tomato-liver mixture. Heat thoroughly and pour over ½ pound cooked *perciatelli*.

Mezzani (medium-size macaroni) with Eggplant: Mezzani is also in the 10-to-14-minute class when it comes to cooking. Prepare ½ pound of medium-size macaroni. Meanwhile, fry thin, peeled slices from a small eggplant in ¼ cup olive oil until golden brown. Set slices aside in a dish as they are browned. Put 1 clove garlic through a press and add to olive oil along with 1 can condensed tomato soup, ½ teaspoon basil and simmer for a few minutes.

Put a third of the macaroni in the bottom of a greased casserole, cover with a layer of eggplant slices (½ of the slices) and sprinkle with grated Parmesan cheese. Repeat. Top with the final layer of macaroni, pour tomato sauce over all, and bake in a moderate oven (350°F.) for 12 minutes.

Elbow Spaghetti with Garlic Sauce: Cook elbow spaghetti for 4 to 6 minutes and drain. In the meantime sauté 4 crushed cloves garlic in ½ cup olive oil until golden; add ½ cup chopped fresh parsley, ¼ teaspoon salt, and a dash of pepper, plus the cooked elbows, and simmer for about 3 minutes or until elbows absorb the sauce.

Mezzani with Wine Sauce: Cook ½ pound cut macaroni (*mezzani*) for 12 to 16 minutes, and drain. Heat 1 cup canned tomato sauce with 1 cup diced cheddar or Bel Paese cheese until smooth. Stir in ¼ cup sherry wine. Put macaroni in heated serving dish, add sauce and toss lightly.

Ziti with Olive Sauce: Large macaroni also termed *ziti*. This is cooked for 12 to 16 minutes, then drained. Meanwhile sauté 1 small, finely chopped onion in 2 tablespoons of olive oil until golden. Add 1 cup tomato sauce, 1 cup chopped ripe olives, and ¼ cup grated Parmesan cheese, and simmer for 10 minutes. Pour sauce over the ziti in a heated dish, tossing lightly.

Ziti with Ham Sauce: Large macaroni takes 10 to 14 minutes to cook. Meanwhile, add 2 cups diced boiled ham to 1 can tomatoes which contain celery, onions, peppers, sugar, and spices. Add 2 tablespoons of butter. Simmer for 10 minutes, adding ½ teaspoon of dried basil or ½ bay leaf. Add to cooked and drained large macaroni, ½ pound, tossing lightly.

Sailor-style Linguine (Macaroni Ribbons): Small macaroni ribbons (linguine) cook in 6 to 8 minutes. While macaroni is boiling, prepare marinara sauce. Fry 1 chopped clove of garlic in ¼ cup of olive oil until golden brown; add ½ can (1 cup) of tomatoes, mashed, ½ teaspoon sugar, and salt and pepper to taste. Simmer for 5 minutes, stirring constantly. Add ¼ teaspoon of thyme, stir, and pour over macaroni. Sprinkle with parsley.

Bavette with Meat Sauce: Medium-size macaroni ribbons are known as *bavette;* cook them 10 minutes. For meat sauce mix 2 cans or jars of junior baby-food beef with 1 can of tomato sauce and 1 beef bouillon cube that has been dissolved in ¼ cup hot water. Add 1 teaspoon of celery salt, 2 tablespoons of chopped fresh parsley. Simmer for 5 minutes. Pour over *bavette*.

Spinach Macaroni Ribbons with Chili Sauce: These take a little longer to cook, 12 to 16 minutes. Cook ½ pound. Heat separately 1 can of chili con carne without beans. Mix the sauce and macaroni together gently before serving or heap chili sauce in a hollowed-out center. For a special touch, rub the serving dish with a bud of garlic before adding macaroni and chili.

Rigati-sausage Casserole: Cook 1 pound of link sausage in a covered pan for 20 minutes or until done; remove sausage. Pour off all but 3 tablespoons of liquid. Add 1 chopped green pepper and 1 small chopped onion and cook for 5 minutes. Add 1 can condensed tomato soup and heat. Meanwhile, cook the cut grooved macaroni known as *mezzani rigati* for 14 minutes. Drain and place in a buttered casserole. Add sauce, stir well, and top with sausage links. Bake in a moderate oven (350°F.) for 30 minutes.

Rigatoni (Large Grooved Macaroni) with Pepperoni: Cook *rigatoni* for 16 to 20 minutes —longer than any other because it is thicker. Meanwhile sauté lightly ½ pound of pepperoni thinly sliced crosswise, and 1 finely chopped onion in 2 tablespoons of cooking fat. Add 1 cup of tomato sauce and simmer for another 10 minutes. Pour sauce over *rigatoni* in a heated serving dish.

Quills with Herb Butter: Quills (*mastacciolini*) cook for 14 to 18 minutes. As soon as you have started the pot to boiling, melt 1 stick (½ cup) butter in another saucepan and steep any suitable combination of herbs in the melted butter for at least 10 minutes. You can buy mixed herbs or mix your own. The rule of thumb is "no less than 3, no more than 7." An easy but flavorful combination would be ½ teaspoon each of finely chopped parsley, chives, and tarragon, or thyme, or chervil. Watercress would make a good fourth. Toss the herb butter lightly with the macaroni on a heated serving plate.

Macaroni Shells in Fried Onion Sauce: Cook 2 cups sliced onions in ¼ cup of melted butter or olive oil in a covered frying pan for 15 minutes over moderate heat. Uncover and let onions brown, adding ¼ teaspoon of salt and a dash of pepper. Meanwhile cook ½ pound of shells or shellettes (*cavatelli*) for 15 to 19 minutes. Drain and toss lightly with the onion sauce.

9 Salads

Olive and Other Oils

Most Italian olive oil available in this country is rather heavy, has a color somewhat like chartreuse and what might be described as a fruity flavor. There are, however, dozens of others, including the light, pale golden, first-pressing virgin olive oil similar to that of Nice in France, perfect for salads and as a seasoning to be passed around the table with antipasto. Certain Italian epicures consider the olive oil of Lucca the best of the crop.

Like wine, olive oil has its good and bad vintage years. In some families, the art of pressing in hand-mills has been handed down through generations. All this is passing very quickly, however. What we get in America now is generally a blend of many seasons and different locales. If you find pure olive oil too strong for your salads, it is a good idea to combine it with peanut oil, safflower, sunflower, or any other bland salad oil.

For general cooking and for mayonnaise, pure olive oil is too much of the good earth! Use a little for tang but be wary. In the north of Italy for sautéeing vegetables and cooking *frittatas* or other such dishes, the olive oil and the butter civilizations, as Mario Pei calls them, merge and they use equal parts of light olive oil and butter, not margarine.

Olive oil presents a storage problem. On the shelf in most kitchens, an open bottle soon goes rancid. Refrigerators are too cool; the olive oil, while not deteriorating in quality, as far as I can discern, gets cloudy. And after too frequent back and forth from table to refrigerator, it does seem to develop an off-taste. What is the answer? Buy small bottles!

Insalata Rinforza

As the name implies, this is a salad to reinforce your energies. It could, when accompanied by bread and cheese, constitute a fine lunch.

1 clove garlic
3 cups fresh cauliflower (1 medium head) or 2 packages frozen cauliflower, cooked, drained, and chilled

1 cup black olives, quartered
Garnish: fillets of anchovies or capers, and pickled peppers
Romaine lettuce, escarole, or a combination to line your best bowl
Italian dressing

Garlic and red hot chili peppers.

Rub a crockery salad bowl with a cut clove of garlic and throw away the garlic. Line with crisp, cold, torn (rather than cut) pieces of romaine lettuce, escarole, or a combination thereof. Pile in the center of the bowl the lightly cooked cauliflower. Cover cauliflower with olives. Garnish with anchovies or capers (drained) and pickled peppers.

Toss with Italian dressing before serving. Serves 6.

Red Kidney Bean Salad

As part of the antipasto or as an accompaniment to meat dishes, red beans—similar to our kidney beans or pinto beans—make a delicious salad. For added heartiness, tuna fish or anchovies may be added.

To crisp the onion rings, let them soak for about 20 minutes in slightly sugared water or equal parts of skim milk and water. Drain well before adding to salad.

2 large (16-oz.) cans red kidney or pinto beans	½ cup olive or salad oil
6 stalks celery, peeled and diced	½ tsp. dried (or 1 tsp. fresh) basil, cut up
1 large red onion (or white sweet onion), sliced and separated into rings	½ tsp. oregano
	½ tsp. salt
	¼ tsp. black pepper
2 cloves garlic	¼ tsp. red chili pepper, ground up (optional)
½ cup red wine vinegar	6 lettuce cups

Drain beans and rinse. Drain again. Combine diced celery, onion rings, and 2 cloves garlic put through the press. Toss all together with the vinegar and oil. Sprinkle with basil and oregano, salt, black pepper, and (if desired) chili pepper. Allow to stand covered in the refrigerator for at least half an hour.

Be sure to stir well before serving. Americans prefer this salad chilled; Europeans often serve it at room temperature. In any case, it seems more attractive to us when presented in crisp lettuce cups.

Variation: White navy beans may be substituted. These are often called Old Woman's Teeth.

Serves 6.

Neapolitan Cauliflower Salad

On the road to Pompeii we stopped at a roadside trattoria where they served a salad of lightly cooked cauliflowerets. When you can get it, use a medium-size cauliflower; off-season try cooking 2 packages frozen cauliflower just about half the time directed on the package. Chill immediately by dumping into ice water, drain and dry.

1 medium-size cauliflower or 2 packages frozen	1 Tbs. capers
	1 small (1¾-oz.) tin anchovy fillets
2 Tbs. olive oil	½ cup sliced black olives
1 Tbs. wine vinegar	
½ tsp. pepper	Lettuce for garnish (Boston or red)

Cook the cauliflower and allow it to cool. Place it in a capacious salad bowl and add the olive oil, 1 Tbs. wine vinegar, ½ tsp. pepper, 1 Tbs. drained capers, 1 small can anchovy fillets, drained, and ½ cup sliced black olives. Toss all together lightly being careful not to break up the cauliflowerets.

Arrange a garland of crisp green, Boston lettuce leaves, if you can't get red lettuce such as we had on the road to Pompeii. Red lettuce, by the way, is available a good part of the year in the western part of the United States but hard to find except in health shops in the east and middle west. Very tender, young red cabbage leaves may be substituted. Serves 6.

Insalata di Funghi
Salad of Raw Mushrooms

The mushrooms available in this country are showy snow-white at their best and have comparatively little taste or fragrance when cooked. They are excellent, however, for raw mushroom salads.

They should be sliced lengthwise through the stem. Washing is usually unnecessary; wipe with a damp towel if you wish. Cut the brown edges off the stem, and unless you are planning to serve the salad within minutes, sprinkle with a little lemon juice to keep them from discoloring.

½ lb. medium-size, firm, white mushrooms	1 head endive
	½ tsp. salt
	¼ tsp. pepper
3 Tbs. lemon juice (juice of 1 lemon)	2 Tbs. peanut oil
	1 good, ripe tomato
1 small clove garlic, peeled and cut in half (optional)	Anchovy fillets (optional)

Slice the mushrooms very thin. Place in a crockery bowl. Sprinkle well with the lemon juice and toss adding, if you wish, the garlic (peeled, cut in half, and held together with a toothpick so that it can be removed at serving time).

Arrange endive fingers on a deepish plate. Sprinkle mushroom salad lightly with about ½ teaspoon of salt and ¼ teaspoon of pepper. Remove garlic. Add peanut oil. Cut tomato into eighths and arrange as a garnish for mushroom salad. If you want to go Genoese, crisscross salad with several anchovy fillets. Serves 4.

Umbrian Potato Salad

Contrary to popular opinion, Italy can produce potatoes almost as tasty as Ireland's. Potatoes are much used not only in northern Italy but also in the central part of the country.

A view of the Bay of Naples, with Mt. Vesuvius in the distance.

Salads

4 large (or 6 medium-size) cold, boiled potatoes
12 radishes
10 stalks lightly cooked asparagus (or 1 package frozen asparagus, cooked)
2 cups cold, cooked green or wax beans
½ cup Italian salad dressing
1 head romaine lettuce

Cube or slice the potatoes. Slice the radishes. Cut asparagus into 1-inch pieces. Combine all these with 2 cups cold, cooked green or wax beans and toss with salad dressing—gently, so as not to mash the potatoes.

Serve surrounded by spikes of romaine lettuce.

Serves 6 as a side dish or 4 for lunch main courses.

Tomatoes Basilica

Now that edible fresh tomatoes are being shipped into this country from Mexico and raised all year round in Florida, California, and Texas, this dish, which is the ultimate in simple saladry, becomes available throughout many months of the year. Provide at least one tomato per person.

Two of the most essential herbs in Italian cooking.

6 good-size fresh, ripe (but not squashy) tomatoes
6 Tbs. fresh basil
6 tsp. wine vinegar
3 tsp. olive oil (optional)

Cut and remove seeds from tomatoes. Peel if you must. Cut into small pieces about ¾ of an inch square. Sprinkle each tomato with 1 tablespoon basil, 1 teaspoon of wine vinegar and half as much olive oil.

Generally salt and pepper are not necessary if the tomatoes are covered and allowed to stand at room temperature for at least half an hour. The basil will provide all the flavoring that is necessary.

In Italy, greenery is not considered necessary with tomatoes *basilica*. They stand on their own, but suit yourself.

Serves 6.

Tuna and Red Bean Salad

Before the American "invasion," salads like these would more than likely have been served as a part of the antipasto. But now in Italy, as well as in our own country, you will find salads doing the honors as a principal dish for lunch. A glass of wine and hot, crusty bread improve the picture enormously.

1 large can red kidney beans or pinto beans, drained
½ cup red wine vinegar
½ tsp. marjoram
1 tsp. fresh parsley, chopped
1 clove garlic
1 medium-size can (about 1 cup) tuna fish
½ cup olive oil
1 scant tsp. salt
¼ tsp. pepper
Crisp romaine lettuce or escarole
3 or 4 anchovy fillets

To the beans add the vinegar, marjoram, chopped parsley, garlic put through the press, tuna fish broken up into large flakes, olive oil, 1 scant teaspoon of salt, ¼ teaspoon of pepper. Mix well and let stand covered in the refrigerator for at least 4 hours.

At serving time, garnish with crisp romaine lettuce or escarole and lay several anchovy fillets on top.

Serves 6.

10
Pizza, Heroes, Sandwiches, and Bread

Basic Pizza Recipe

Any good white bread dough made with yeast can be used for making a pizza. However, the authentic recipe is made without any shortening or sugar. The recipe that we got in Naples calls for 100 grams of white flour mixed with 50 grams of water, a pinch of salt, and a pinch of yeast. Knead well. Then cut the dough into small, round loaves and place in a kneading trough to rise. The kneading is usually done at night. During the day the loaves are brought to the marble-topped bench where they are vigorously kneaded once again and finally rolled out to the necessary size.

> 1 package dry yeast ½ tsp. salt
> 2 cups sifted white flour

Soften the dry yeast in ½ cup of warm water. Then add it, with ½ teaspoon of salt, to the flour. Mix and knead with your hands until you have a smooth dough. Set aside, covered, to rise until it has doubled in bulk (about 1 hour). Roll or stretch the dough on a floured board or marble slab until it is less than ½ inch thick. Fit into pie pans or a pizza pan or lay on a cookie sheet. Cover with the desired ingredients.

Bake in the hottest oven you can achieve; 550°F. is recommended. (It is practically impossible to get the oven as hot as the true pizza maker would like.) A pizza should be baked in about 8 minutes. The dough should be very thin and brown and crisp, but not burned.

Serve fiery hot with red wine or beer, or hot coffee. This amount makes 1 pizza, about 12 inches in diameter; or 2 pie-sized pizzas.

No lard or fat is used by the classic pizza makers of Naples in making their dough. However, if you want a more tender crust, you may add 1 tablespoon lard or vegetable shortening to the basic pizza dough ingredients. Serves 6.

The Pizza Margherita

This pizza, probably the most famous of them all, combines the flavor of tomato with mozzarella, a soft cheese made traditionally in Italy of buffalo milk, but quite untraditionally of cow's milk all over the world. According to

Pizza as it's baked in Naples.

tradition, Esposito was the inventor of the Margherita pizza. In 1889 an official of the royal establishment went expressly to his famous pizzeria to ask him to go immediately to the royal residence and give his sovereigns a demonstration of his skill. For his royal clients on that occasion he prepared various pizzas; all, according to history, exquisitely flavored, the borders of dough exceedingly thin and crisp. The queen at that time expressed preference for the pizza garnished with mozzarella and tomato. So this personal creation of Esposito was christened Margherita and was used to celebrate the visit to Naples of King Umberto's consort, Queen Margherita.

The pizza Margherita is garnished with thin slices of mozzarella cheese, sprinkled with finely chopped fresh basil (or about ¼ teaspoon dry basil rubbed between the hands to release the oils). Top with a purée of tomatoes and sprinkle with grated sharp cheese like Parmesan or Romano.

Pizza with anchovies: Fresh anchovies or anchovy fillets in oil are used to decorate but not entirely cover the dough. Sprinkle lightly with crushed or finely minced garlic and a generous amount of fresh or dried marjoram. Anoint generously with olive oil.

Pizza bella napoli: Here the pizza is divided into four quarters. The first quarter is sprinkled with capers, stoned black olives, and anchovies. Anchovies wrapped around capers are often used. Second quarter: tiny clams or Neapolitan cockles. Often these are placed on the dough in their shells. Third quarter: mussels. Fourth quarter: mushrooms, bottled in oil. Garnish the center with a round piece of mozzarella.

Cossack pizza: Only tomato and grated Parmesan and Romano cheese are used in this version. No herbs or garlic.

Pizza four seasons: In this case the pizza is divided into four quarters. One quarter is scattered with chopped clams or Neapolitan cockles. The second quarter uses chopped mussels. The third quarter is covered with 5 small, pickled artichokes, and the fourth with 5 black olives from which the stones have been removed.

The divisions are made with fillets of anchovies.

Pizza frattese: This pizza was invented by a master from the town of Fratte in the Pesaro province who came to Naples to learn his craft. In his version of the pizza the dough is covered solidly with cheese—any preferred cheese may be used—and then it is sprinkled with olive oil. Tomato may be used but it is not necessary. Actually this is quite similar to our own cheese dream.

Pizza with mushrooms: The dough is brushed with olive oil, lightly sprinkled with fine crushed or minced garlic, and covered with a handful of fresh mushrooms (or dried Italian mushrooms, soaked in warm water, then drained and coarsely cut up). The mushrooms should be brushed well with oil so that they do not shrivel in the heat of the oven.

Pizza pasqualino: The son of one of Naples' famous chefs is said to have been the first to divide the pizza into four sections. The first section is covered with shrimp and fried octopus cut into bits; or, if you have no octopus on hand, shrimp can be used alone. The second section is devoted to tomato and anchovies (in Naples fresh anchovies are used, but fillets will do very well). The third section is the classic Margherita combination: mozzarella, tomato, Parmesan, and basil leaves. The fourth is alla Romano—mozzarella, anchovies, tomato, marjoram, and pepper. As a final touch, in the center there is an egg in its own shell placed on the dough and cooked by the heat of the oven—a roasted egg.

Pizza Porta San Gennaro: This is the plainest and most elementary of all pizzas. The recipe calls for an *ombra* (a veil or a shadow) of finely cut parsley, 2 basil leaves finely cut, and 1 fresh, firm, sliced tomato. There is no oil, no pepper. Only a pinch of the coarse salt of Naples.

Roman pizza: Cover the dough with thin strips of mozzarella. Sprinkle with pepper and fresh or dried marjoram (use about ¼ teaspoon of dry marjoram or about ¾ teaspoon of fresh marjoram). Top with fresh tomato purée and decorate with 2 or 3 anchovy fillets.

Pizza alla marinara: In Naples we were warned "to give no credence to those people who tell you that *pizza alla marinara* is not the original classical and traditional Neapolitan pizza." It is regarded as the forerunner of all pizzas. Please, they begged, give the old ancestor the honor due to it.

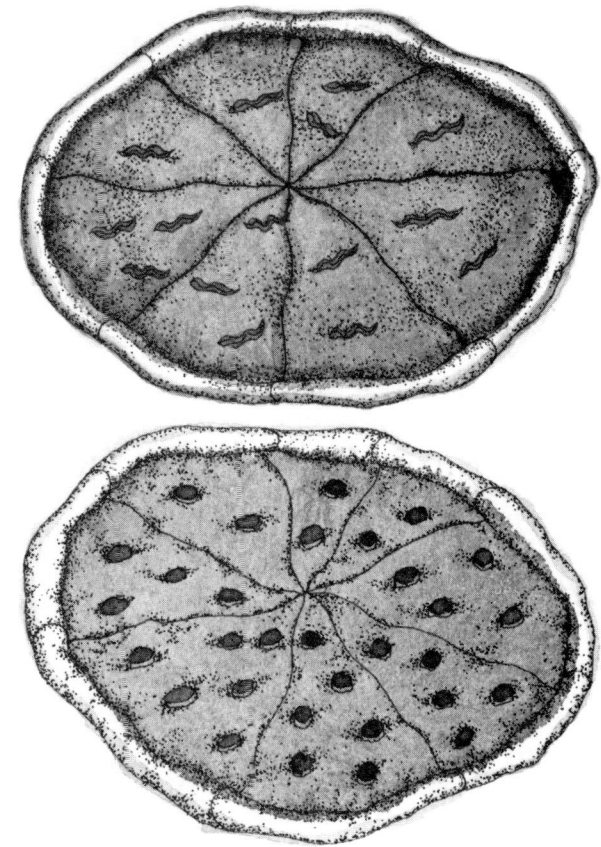

Pizza, Heroes, Sandwiches, and Bread

To make the classic *pizza alla marinara*, you must have the basic pizza dough which is rolled out into a thin circle and is called a *pettola*, which is translated as a piece of white linen but more accurately means a shirttail.

Oregano may be used instead of marjoram. As a matter of fact, the two herbs seem to be used almost interchangeably in Italian cooking.

Basic pizza dough (see page 61)
1 clove garlic
Marjoram or oregano
Purée of tomatoes

Roll the dough as thin as possible. Sprinkle very lightly with finely crushed garlic put through a press or cut with a chef's knife into the smallest possible pieces. Sprinkle with fresh or finely powdered marjoram, using just enough to dot the dough ever so lightly. Then add enough purée of tomatoes to make a light covering.

Bake in a hot, hot oven, preheated to 550°F.

To serve, break into pieces or cut into wedges while pizza is still as hot as can be handled.

Calzoni
Trouser Legs

In many pizzerias and also often in the *rosticerrie*, which are a kind of combination rotisserie and cafeteria, they often serve a folded-over pizza that is dropped into hot fat and fried, rather than baked in the oven. Just as they come from the kettle, they have the blown-up look of sailor pants in the breeze.

This hearty and filling provender can be made with any of the garnishes used for a flat pizza, but generally slices of mozzarella and often bits of ham are used. In Italy, they are usually about 8 inches in diameter; but here in America you might like to try a smaller version and, if you wish, you could use a ready-to-serve biscuit for the dough.

Basic pizza dough (See page 61) *or*
1 package refrigerated biscuit dough
3 Tbs. olive oil
8 slices mozzarella or other mild white cheese, thinly sliced
½ cup diced, cooked ham or prosciutto
¼ tsp. pepper
½ tsp. dried oregano or marjoram (optional)
Oil for frying

Roll dough or pat refrigerated biscuit dough into circles about 4 inches in diameter. Brush with olive oil. Arrange cheese. Sprinkle with finely diced ham or prosciutto. Sprinkle with a few grains of pepper and, if you wish, a little dried oregano or marjoram, rubbed between the fingers to release the oils. Press the two sides together with the tines of a fork. Be sure that the olive oil extends to the edges for it helps to hold the circle together.

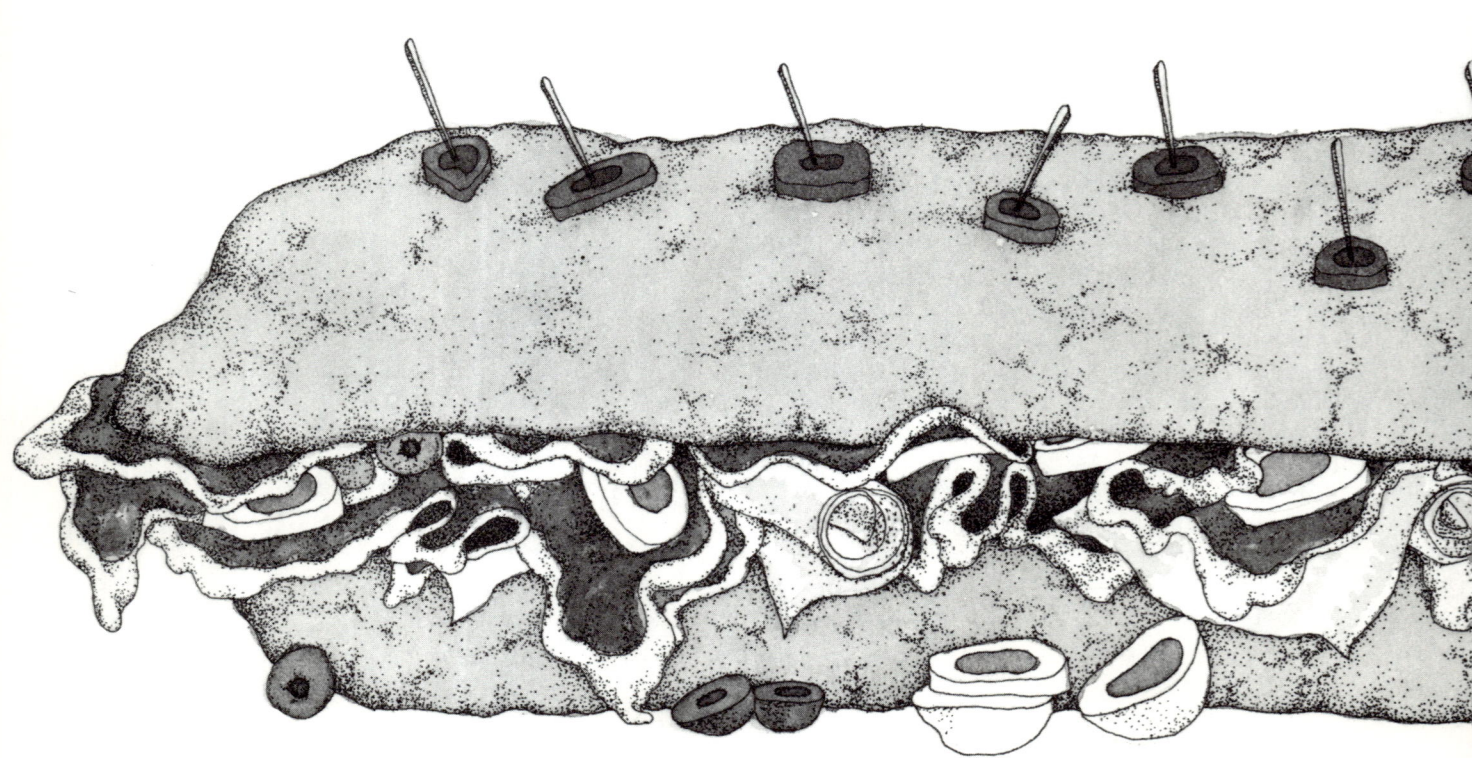

Drop two or three at a time into deep hot oil (370°F.) and cook for about 3 minutes or until golden brown. Drain on paper towels.

Be sure that they are still puffy and hot. Serve with a salad and cooked green vegetables and red wine or beer.
Serves 8.

Six-foot Hero Sandwich

To tell the truth, I never saw a six-foot hero sandwich in any part of Italy, nor even a hero sandwich as such—just hunks of bread with various fillings. However, like the pizza, the hero has become an Italian-American institution. To the best of our knowledge the creation dates back to Manganaro's, a famous Italian shop on Ninth Avenue in New York. In those days given sufficient notice of 3 or 4 days, they could be induced—at a price—to deliver their prodigious creations within the city limits Mondays through Fridays.

You might want to use a method we evolved for producing them ourselves using long loaves of crusty Italian bread. This, of course, is party food designed for about 32 people.

6 long loaves crusty Italian bread, about 4 inches wide	1 lb. cooked ham, thinly sliced
Butter for spreading	2 lbs. Italian cheese, sliced
1 lb. bologna or salami	etc., for garnish
Sliced olives, pimiento strips, cole slaw,	Lettuce and tomato (optional)

Cut both ends off 4 loaves and leave 1 end apiece on 2 other loaves. Fit together end-to-end so that you seem to have one long, long loaf. Then cut loaves crosswise all the way through and hollow them out a little so that you don't have too much bread. Soften butter and smoothly spread both sides of the bread. Cover the bottom of one section with thinly sliced salami or bologna overlapping generously. Cover the next section with sliced cheese, the next with thinly sliced ham. Garnish with sliced olives, strips of pimiento, well drained cole slaw or vegetable antipasto or any other sliced pickles or pickled vegetables. Tomato slices and lettuce should be used only when you plan to eat the sandwich rather promptly. Press the 2 halves together.

Cut into sections from 2 to 4 inches wide, depending upon the size of your loaf.
Serves 32.

Sicilian Sandwiches Guastiedde

Not too well known in the States up to now, a hearty sandwich fresh from Sicily that has the affectionate nickname of *guastiedde*—a jolly good fellow.

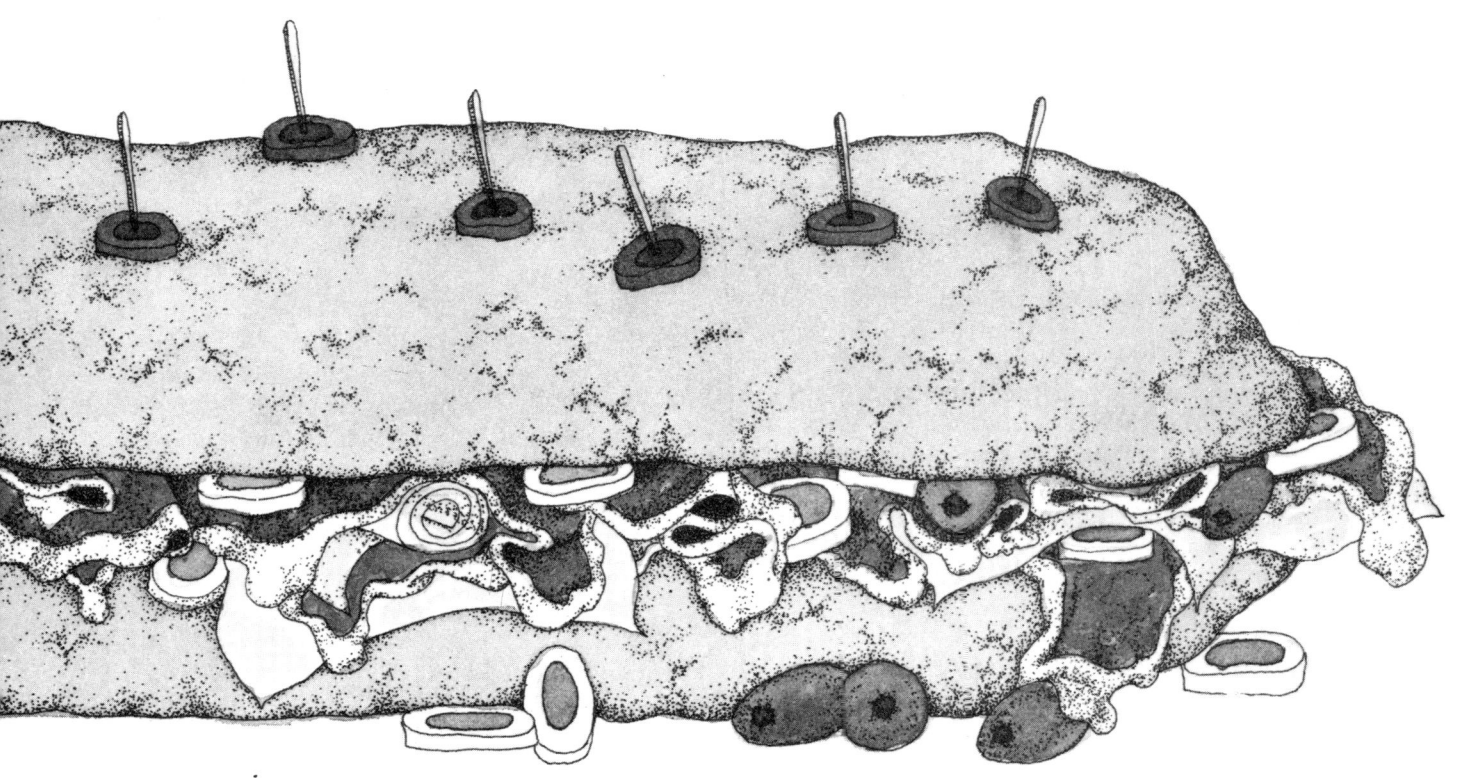

Pizza, Heroes, Sandwiches, and Bread

Essentially the *guastiedde* is a hot sausage and melted cheese sandwich served in a large soft roll that is like an oversize hamburger bun. The principal ingredients are peppery sausages fried and cut into slices, combined with a layer of Italian ricotta (or creamed cottage cheese) and slices of mozzarella, which might be replaced by a mild muenster or Monterey Jack cheese.

1½ lbs. Italian sausage	1 lb. ricotta or an equal amount creamy cottage cheese
6 large hamburger-type buns	6 slices mozzarella, muenster, or Monterey Jack cheese, cut ¼-inch thick

Fry sausage until well cooked and lightly browned. Remove from pan. Drain (saving the drippings) and cut into slices about ¼ inch thick. Cut 6 large hamburger-type buns in half crosswise. Cover the bottom half with a layer of sliced fried sausage, then a layer (about ¼ inch thick) of ricotta or creamy cottage cheese. Cover the ricotta with a layer of mozzarella cheese (or muenster or Monterey Jack), also cut ¼ inch thick. Sprinkle with 1 teaspoon of the sausage drippings. Replace top on the roll; wrap each one separately in foil. Place in a moderately hot oven (375°F.) for 10 to 12 minutes or until the bread is thoroughly warmed and the cheese lusciously melted.

Serve in the foil.
Serves 6.

Introduction to Italian Bread

In San Francisco and a few places in New York you may still be able to find some real Italian bread but it is rarer than white truffles. Italian bread differs from French not only in the quality and color of the grain but because it has in most regions of Italy a definite sour dough quality. It is made from yeast that does not come in cakes or packets. Usually it is "borrowed" in the villages from a neighbor who has just finished making up her batch of bread and always has some dough left over. Consequently, the yeast, like that of our own salt-rising bread in the South, comes from the wild yeast in the air. It has all the mysterious quality of the treasured yeast used in making sour mash bourbon and precious malt whiskeys.

Sour dough starter may be secured from Alaska, where it is still highly esteemed for pancakes as well as biscuits and bread. And you can, if you like, make your own starter and keep it alive in the refrigerator or freezer for months at a time. But all this is a special hobby.

What we offer here is an Italian bread made without milk, which is traditional, and using honey instead of sugar.

If you have trouble finding a place that is just about right for letting the dough rise—a little higher than body temperature—turn on your oven to 350°F. for 1 minute and then turn it off. That minute of heat, plus the pilot light, gives you a wonderful draft-free haven for your bread. It does away with the use of a featherbed or pillows such as they used in the farmhouses of older times.

Pepper bread.

Sesame-seeded Italian Bread

This is a simple light-colored bread that can be shaped into round or oblong loaves. Unlike typical French bread, it contains a small amount of oil, which keeps it from going stale so fast.

2¼ cups lukewarm water	6 cups enriched sifted flour

1 Tbs. salt
2 Tbs. clover honey or sugar
2 cakes yeast
2 Tbs. butter, softened, or oil
1 cup toasted wheat germ
1 egg white (optional)
Sesame seeds

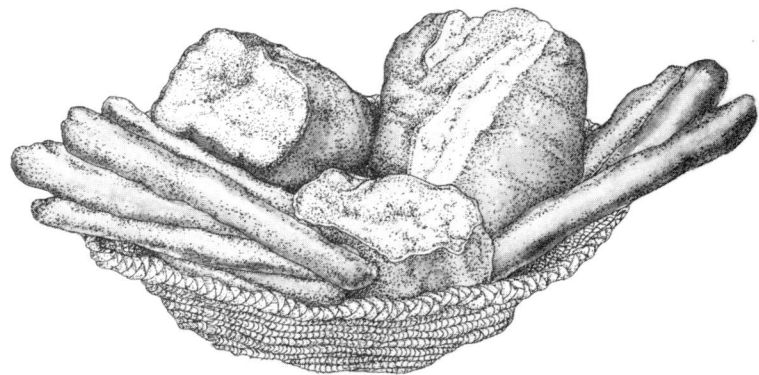

In a large bowl, combine lukewarm water, 1 tablespoon of salt, and the honey or sugar, and mix well. Crumble in the yeast; stir until yeast is dissolved. Add butter, softened, or oil; gradually mix in half of the flour with a wooden spoon. Mix well; add balance of flour and wheat germ and mix with hands. When dough leaves sides of bowl, turn it out on a lightly floured board and knead for about 10 minutes. Place in greased bowl; brush top lightly with a little additional shortening or oil; cover bowl with damp towel and set aside in warm place to rise until doubled, about 1½ hours.

Then punch down; fold dough over and turn it completely over in the bowl. Let it rise again, covered, until almost doubled, about 45 minutes.

Divide dough in half; cover and set aside for 10 minutes. On a board, flatten dough with hands into oblong shapes; fold over in half and flatten again. Gently roll each piece with hands and shape into round or oblong loaf. Place in greased pans, or on a large shallow baking sheet that has been sprinkled with cornmeal. Set aside in warm place to rise for 30 minutes, uncovered, then brush with cold water. Make quarter-inch-deep diagonal slashes in the dough and set aside for about 15 minutes.

For crisp crust brush with egg white diluted with water. Sprinkle thickly with sesame seeds and bake in a preheated 400°F. oven for 30 minutes or until bread is nicely browned and loaf when tapped sounds hollow. Remove from pan and place on wire rack to cool away from drafts.

Makes 2 large loaves.

Pepper Bread

In the province of Puglia, they make a surprising bread that includes a tablespoon of cracked black pepper and a couple of slices of crisp, crumbled bacon.

1 package dry yeast
½ cup dry milk
5½ cups sifted flour
1 tsp. salt
1 Tbs. cracked black pepper
½ tsp. dry basil
3 Tbs. lard, softened
2 slices bacon
Melted butter

Dissolve yeast in ¼ cup of warm water. In a bowl, combine the salt, pepper, basil, milk, and 2 cups of flour. Add lard and 1½ cups water. Brown bacon, crumble and add. Mix with a large spoon or fork. Add yeast and mix until smooth.

Add 3½ cups flour to make a fairly stiff dough, turn out on a lightly floured board, and knead for about 8 minutes or until smooth and elastic.

Place the dough in a greased bowl and brush top with melted butter or lard. Cover

The glory of fresh-baked bread.

Pizza, Heroes, Sandwiches, and Bread

with damp cloth and set aside in warm place until double its bulk, about 1 hour. Punch down. Shape into a round loaf and place in a large, greased, round bread pan or cake pan; cover and set aside until double its bulk, about 1 hour. Brush top with melted butter.

Bake in a preheated 425°F. oven for 15 minutes; lower temperature to 375°F. and bake 25 minutes longer or until bread shrinks from sides of pan is nicely browned.
Makes 1 loaf.

Polenta

Polenta is yellow cornmeal mush made of yellow maize flour and a staple in the diet of northern Italy. Made with or without cheese, it often takes the place of bread, especially in the less affluent households.

There was once an edict that all meal must be added practically grain by grain to the rapidly boiling water and stirred in, so that *polenta* would not end up lumpy.

But we discovered down South and in our own Middle West that many cooks prevented lumps by mixing the meal with a cup of cold water and then adding it to the boiling salted water. No lumps ever and the taste was amazingly good. There are various types of *polenta* —coarse and fine, white and yellow.

| 1 cup yellow quick-cooking cornmeal | ½ cup grated cheese (optional) |
| Salt | ½ cup butter (optional) |

Mix cornmeal with 1 cup cold water and add to 4 to 5 cups rapidly boiling salted water, depending upon how thick you want your mush. Stir with a notched stick or wooden spoon until it is a thick, smooth mass. Add grated cheese or butter. (The old-fashioned cornmeal or *polenta* took about 20 minutes to cook. Many brands now on the market cook much faster.)

Plain *polenta* is traditionally served in a circle of tablespoonfuls around roasted small birds, fried liver, or codfish. Contrary to popular opinion, it can be reheated and you don't need a double-boiler, either. Just add a little warm water and stir.
Serves 4 to 6.

Two ways to serve polenta.

11
Dessert and Coffee

Frittata Fruttata

A *frittata* is an omelet (see page 36).

This dessert omelet is served from its own baking dish in wedges.

A maverick in several ways, our *frittata*, like a soufflé, begins with a cream sauce base. But you make the sauce with cold rather than hot milk so that there are no chances for lumps. It is silky-smooth.

The original Palermo recipe calls for apricot purée but we substitute baby-food apricots or apricots and applesauce as a covering for mixed frozen fruits.

Use a flame-proof skillet with a nonflammable handle, attractive enough to appear at the table.

1 Tbs. butter	¼ tsp. cinnamon
1 Tbs. flour	1 package frozen mixed fruit
2 cups cold milk	1 can baby-food apricots
4 egg yolks	2 Tbs. sugar
5 egg whites, well beaten	¼ cup kirsch or white rum
¼ tsp. salt	(optional)

Grease sides as well as bottom of flame-proof skillet with butter or margarine. On top of stove, melt 1 tablespoon of butter. When foamy, stir in 1 tablespoon of flour and mix well for about 1 minute. Off heat, add cold milk (this breaks all the rules, but works like magic). Cook and stir until thick and silky-smooth. Off heat again, beat in, one by one, 4 egg yolks. Fold in 5 well-beaten egg whites, working lightly. Add ¼ teaspoon each of salt and cinnamon. Cook on top of the stove over moderate heat or cook in moderately hot oven (375°F.) for about 12 minutes or until quite firm.

Meanwhile quick-thaw the frozen mixed fruits so that fruit can be separated. Drain (drink the delicious juices!). Cover *frittata* with fruits. Over all spread lightly the apricot purée. Sprinkle with sugar. Now, if you like, though it isn't necessary, warm the kirsch or white rum in a ramekin to body heat, about 100°F. Set liquor aflame and pour over *frittata*. Set under broiler just long enough to develop a light crust and a glaze.

A market in Padua.

Cut into wedges and serve warm from baking dish. This creation is much easier to do than to describe. It has none of the hazards of a soufflé or an omelet.
Serves 6 to 8.

Petal-thin Fritter Batter

In Italy deep frying is an important procedure. Formerly it was done in olive oil where the temperature could be judged by a haze. Now salad oil is preferred and the thermostatically controlled skillet takes the place of the old-fashioned kettle, drainer, and other paraphernalia.

Fritters made of fruits, like bananas, oranges, pineapple chunks, apples, peaches, and apricots require a batter much lighter than that used for *fritto misto*.

This one makes a very thin, delicate coating and is best made in a blender, though it can be done with a wooden spoon.

2 eggs	¼ tsp. salt
2 tsp. sugar	1 cup sifted, all-purpose flour
1 cup milk	Vegetable oil for frying
1 tsp. salad oil	
1 Tbs. brandy or a dash of lemon juice	

Place in blender the eggs, sugar, milk, salad oil, brandy or lemon juice, and ¼ teaspoon of salt. Blend for about 15 seconds. Add flour and blend for only a second or two until mixed.

If you are not using a blender, make a well in the center of the flour mixed with sugar and salt, and add the other ingredients. Stir with a wooden spoon or a fork. The batter should not be worked too much.

If possible, it is best to let your batter stand uncovered for half an hour at room temperature before using it. If you desire, you may separate the eggs and add the stiffly beaten whites to the mixture just before dipping the fruits into it. The mixture should then be thick as whipping cream.
Makes 1½-2 cups.

Tangerine or Orange Fritters

Although all sorts of fruits are used, we will choose as an example two of the most popular, the tangerine and orange. Fresh fruit may be used, of course, but canned mandarin or orange sections will do admirably.

6 tangerines or oranges or 1 can mandarin orange sections	Flour
	Sugar
	Vanilla, lemon, or eggnog sauce (optional)
3 Tbs. lime or lemon juice	Vegetable oil for frying
Petal-thin fritter batter	

Break tangerines or oranges into sections if you are using fresh fruit; if using canned mandarin sections, sprinkle with lime or lemon juice, and let stand for about 15 minutes; drain again and dry on paper towels so that the fritters will stay crispy.

Flour fruit for fritters lightly. Then dip into petal-thin fritter batter (see page 71), allowing batter to drip through the tines of a fork. Drop a few at a time into vegetable oil heated to 370°F. Cook for about 3 minutes until golden brown.

Sprinkle with sugar or serve with a vanilla, lemon, or eggnog sauce.
Serves 6-8.

An antique pewter pitcher for sauces.

Dessert and Coffee

Bananas of the Bronze Horse

A few years ago, in the city of Turin in the northern province of Piedmont, there was a *birreria* (beergarden) that nobody forgets—the *birreria* of the Bronze Horse. Most famous not for beer, but for bananas cooked in a special way.

So dramatic, so different, the bananas of the Bronze Horse can transform the most impromptu supper into a memorable occasion.

4 Tbs. butter	6 good-size bananas, cut into 1″ chunks
½ cup sugar	
4 thin strips lemon rind	12 pitted dates, cut in quarters
	Plain or whipped cream (optional)

Melt the butter in an electric skillet or wide frying pan. Add sugar, ¼ cup of water, lemon rind, and cut-up pitted dates. Cook until mixture takes on the pale hue and look of caramel syrup. Add the 1-inch chunks of bananas. Carefully turn the pieces from time to time so that all are well and evenly cooked, but not soft. Serve with plain or whipped cream. Serves 6 to 8.

Baked Peaches Italienne

Use fresh, large peaches that are not too ripe, when available. Canned peach halves make an excellent substitute.

1 large can of peach halves or 7 fresh whole peaches	½ tsp. almond extract
	1 tsp. grated lemon or orange rind
½ cup toasted almonds or other nuts, finely chopped	4 ladyfingers
	¼ cup white wine
	¼ cup white or brown sugar

Drain a large can of peach halves. Place 6 on a buttered baking pan, preferably one that can come to the table. Make the stuffing for the peaches by mashing together 2 peach halves, chopped nuts, almond extract, a bit of grated lemon or orange rind, and the ladyfingers cut into very fine pieces. If the mixture is not moist enough to hold together, add a couple of teaspoons of peach syrup from the can. Form into balls about the size of a peach pit.

Baked stuffed peaches with macaroons.

Cassata.

Place in the peaches and cover with other peach halves so that the peaches look whole. Pour wine over them. Sprinkle with sugar. Bake in a moderate oven for about 10 minutes or until the sugar has formed a pretty crust.

Serve warm or cold.
Serves 6.
Variation: Baked Stuffed Peaches with Macaroons. In the above recipe use 8 macaroons instead of ladyfingers and omit the almond extract.

Cassata
Sicilian Cream Cheese Cake

For festive occasions this famous and lusciously rich icebox cake from Sicily deserves a great American revival. It is a perfect party specialty. We should warn you, however, that when you see *cassata* on a menu in other parts of Italy or in the United States, it is usually ice cream; often an elaborate spumoni.

1 lb. Italian ricotta or creamy cottage cheese	2 Tbs. chocolate bits or diced candied fruits
2 cups sugar	4 layers sponge or pound cake, each ½-inch thick
1 tsp. vanilla	
3 Tbs. *crème de cacao* liqueur	Confectioners' sugar

Place ricotta or any other creamy cottage cheese into a large bowl along with the sugar, vanilla, and *crème de cacao* liqueur. Mix well until smooth and fluffy. With the traditional long-handled wooden spoon, it takes about 10 minutes to achieve the proper degree of fluffiness. A mixer does it in 2 or 3 minutes. Now stir in the chocolate bits or diced candied fruits, any kind you like. This is the filling for your icebox cake.

Cut sponge cake layers or any sponge cake or pound cake into slices ½-inch thick and cover the bottom and sides of a straightsided casserole with the cake. Pour the cream mixture into the center. Cover the top with more sliced cake, crust side up, and let stand in the refrigerator overnight.

Turn out on chilled serving dish and sprinkle with confectioners' sugar. You will want to serve only small wedges as this cake is quite rich.
Serves 12.

Frozen Tangerines of Milan

Discovered in Milan: a practically perfect answer to the dinner-party dessert problem. Excellent for buffet service. A fine delicacy to keep on hand in the freezer for emergencies.

Frozen tangerines of Milan.

Dessert and Coffee

6 or 8 tangerines or oranges
1 quart orange- or tangerine-flavored sherbet or ice cream for filling
6 green leaves for garnish
aurum or *mandarino* (tangerine liqueur) (optional)

Cut off tops and carefully remove fruit from solid tangerines or small oranges, leaving shell intact. Make or buy 1 quart orange- or tangerine-flavored sherbet or ice cream. Fill shells. Replace tops to make a lid. Place on a tray. If you wish, this may be kept in the freezing compartment from 1 to 3 hours.

If too hard-frozen, allow to stand for ½ hour in the refrigerator or for about 10 minutes at room temperature. With a toothpick stick a green leaf into the top of each tangerine. If you wish you may remove the lid. Make a little hole in the sherbet and pour on about a tablespoon of an appropriately flavored liqueur—like the Italian *aurum* ("of oranges") or *mandarino*, a tangerine liqueur.
Serves 6.

Ricotta Condita

One of the greatest Italian desserts in the world and certainly one of the simplest is made of ricotta. It is now available in supermarkets everywhere, probably because it is now made from regular milk instead of the original buffalo milk and later ewe's milk.

2 Tbs. cream
2 cups Italian ricotta or cottage cheese
2 Tbs. sugar
2 Tbs. rum
Cinnamon

Add the cream to Italian ricotta or creamed cottage cheese, the sugar, and rum. Blend or beat until very smooth. Serve in a chilled bowl. Sprinkle lightly with cinnamon.

Serve with heated coffee cake or quick-frozen cinnamon nut loaf in thin slices. Even more luscious, serve it with whole strawberries, peaches, or apricots—preferably fresh, though frozen will do, especially quick-thawed.
Serves 6.

Italian Walnut Torta

One of the memorable meals of his life, according to our favorite editor who traveled through Italy armed with some of our recipes and tasting suggestions, was a *torta* or gargantuan cookie found in a bake shop in Bologna and eaten at sunset along the road. This is a simplified homemade version that always brings back the memories of that enchanted evening.

1¼ cups walnuts, finely ground
¾ cup sugar
⅓ cup unsweetened cocoa
4 eggs, separated
1 tsp. vanilla extract
1 tsp. grated lemon rind
2 Tbs. bread crumbs

Combine the ground (or blended) walnuts with sugar and cocoa. Gradually add 4 very well-beaten egg yolks, vanilla extract, and grated lemon rind. Beat 4 egg whites until stiff but not dry and fold into the mixture carefully. Butter a 9-inch glass baking dish; dust with bread crumbs. Bake in a 350°F. oven for 30 minutes or until cake tester comes out clean.

This is usually served in Italy with a sweet dessert wine such as Marsala.
Makes 12 portions. However, don't count on it for more than 4 or 5 people—it's that good!

Zuppa Inglese con Frutta

The classic *zuppa inglese* ("English soup") obviously came to Italy with the influx of Edwardian travelers in the days when the Grand Tour was part of the education of English romantics. It used to be a tipsy pudding made with custard and covered with meringue, often laid on in elaborate designs. Now the rich *zuppa* is rarely encountered except at baptismal feasts and in some of the popular tourist restaurants.

1 layer of sponge cake
½ cup rum
2 packages quick-thaw mixed frozen fruit or 2 cans chilled, mixed fruit salad (large pieces, not like fruit cocktail)
1 pint ice cream

Cut a layer of sponge cake in half crosswise. Sprinkle the cut sides with rum. Drain the mixed fruit and place it between the layers and on top of the cake. The dessert may be served within half an hour but it is better if allowed to stand in the refrigerator for several hours.

Cut into wedges and top with a scoop of ice cream.
Serves 6 to 8.

Caffè Filtrato

Almost as popular as espresso coffee is *caffè filtrato*, also called *caffè a macchinetta*. An espresso machine is extremely complicated, but a *macchinetta*, in spite of its name, is anything but mechanical. It is merely a two-part coffee pot equipped with two spouts and two handles. One part is equipped with a cuplike sieve rather like the basket in a percolator. These come in all sizes, all prices, and are made in all materials.

Use dark roast coffee, very finely ground—a drip grind. Italian or French roast coffee can be bought anywhere in any city in the United States.

Follow directions given with your machine for amounts of coffee and water to use.

Fill the cup or basket of the *macchinetta* no more than ¾ full with coffee; the coffee expands, so it should not be too full. Place the required amount of boiling water in the lower part of the *macchinetta* and put the whole thing over low heat. Wait for the little hole in the lower cylinder to begin to spurt; then, protecting your hands with a towel, quickly turn the whole thing upside down. You will hear the coffee begin to drip. When the dripping stops, it is time to serve.

Always provide a piece of lemon rind and sugar for those who want it. Cream is never used.

Granita di Caffè

A granita is a kind of half-frozen sherbet and the *granita di caffè* is the most popular in Italy. In cafés and sidewalk carts, it is a snack served plain and in homes, at dessert time, it is often topped with slightly sweetened or liqueur-flavored whipped cream.

The classic zuppa inglese, which is not a soup, but a rich cake for special occasions.

¾ cup sugar
4 level tsp. instant espresso coffee
¼ cup whipped cream or topping
1 Tbs. *crème de cacao* or *anisette* (optional)

Add the sugar to 4 cups of water in a saucepan. Bring to a boil and cook until bubbling and clear. Stir in coffee. Cool a little so as not to ruin the lining of your ice trays. Then pour into ice trays and place in the freezing compartment at the lowest temperature, stirring every now and then, until the *granita* becomes not solid or hard but just pleasantly mushy. This should take about an hour. If the granita becomes too solid, allow it to stand at room temperature for a few minutes.

Pile into chilled wine or champagne glasses. Top with sweetened whipped cream or topping. Serve with *crème de cacao* or *anisette*, if desired.
Serves 6 to 8.

Caffè Diavolo

Make Italian drip coffee or, if you are lazy, use instant espresso, making it double strength. A very good way to get flavor into instant espresso is to add the required amount of coffee to cold water, not boiling water, and do it in a pot. Bring to a boil and allow to simmer at least 30 seconds. This different technique makes a remarkable change in the flavor.

However you make your coffee, be sure that it is very strong and boiling hot. Warm your cups, or if you prefer to go Italian, your small tumblers or parfait glasses. Fill cups or glasses three-quarters full of the coffee, pouring the coffee onto a silver spoon to prevent glass or fine china from cracking.

A pretty, hand-painted espresso cup.

Slightly warm cognac or brandy in a copper or silver mug and pour enough cognac or brandy into the coffee so that it is almost ready to overflow. Place a match to each cup and let it flame. Or pour a little of the warmed brandy into the teaspoon, light the liquor in the teaspoon, and lower it gradually into the coffee as you pour in more brandy.

To get the full effect, all the lights should be turned low so that the flame will be a bright, brilliant blue like a faraway light in a dark tunnel.

Spring on the Spanish Steps in Rome.

Index

Anchovies
    with broiled peppers, 12–13
    in pizza toppings, 62
Antipasto, 7–8
Artichoke hearts
    batter-fried (*fritto misto*), 31
    in pizza topping, 63
    stuffing for tomatoes, 13

Bananas of the Bronze Horse, 72
Basil, 15–16
    Genoese spaghetti sauce, 53–54
    pesto, 15–16
    pizza seasoning, 62–63
Beans, red kidney, salads of, 58, 60
Beef
    boiled slices with green sauce, 27–28
    chopped, in rice balls, 40
    Neapolitan ragout, 26
    osso buco, 34–35
    pickled, 27–28
    steak *carpaccio*, 9
Bread, Italian, 66
    sesame-seeded, 66–67
    pepper, 67–68

Carrots
    with garlic butter, 44
    marinated, 8–10
Cauliflower
    salads, 57–58
    sauce for *linguine*, 51

Cheese
    crustini, 11
    four-faced pasta, 54–55
    Italian varieties listed, 40–43
    mozzarella "in a carriage," 11–12
    omelet, Italian-style, 36–37
    in pizza toppings, 62–64
    risotto Milanese, 39
    Roman rice balls, 38–39
    in sandwiches, 65–66
Chicken
    with rosemary, 28
    tunnied, 28
Chickpeas (*céci*), salad, 10
Clams
    baked seafood Vesuvio, 23–24
    in pizza toppings, 62, 63
    sauces, 22–23, 51–52
Cornmeal mush (*polenta*), 68

Desserts
    bananas of the Bronze Horse, 72
    "English soup" with fruit, 75–76
    frozen tangerines (oranges), 73–74
    fruit fritters, 71; omelet, 69, 71
    granita di caffè (sherbet), 75–76
    peaches, baked, 72–73
    ricotta condita, 74
    Sicilian cream cheese cake, 73
    walnut *torta*, 74

Eggplant
    baked, with *mezzani*, 55
    marinara, 44–45

Eggs
  baked Florentine-style, 38
  omelets, 36–37, 69
  soups with, 17–20
  spaghetti *alla carbonara*, 53

Fennel (*finocchio*), 11, 28
Fish and seafood:
  baked seafood Vesuvio, 23–24
  barbecued fish, 20–22
  batter-fried, 30–31
  breaded fish sticks, 21
  broiled fillets of sole, 24
  clam sauces, 22–24, 51–57
  crab meat Grand Canal, 10–11
  green sauce for, 20
  lobster *alla diavolo*, 22
  perch with clam sauce, 22–23
  in pizza toppings, 62–63
  shrimp. *See* Shrimp
  stew, 17
  tuna. *See* Tuna
Fruit. *See* Desserts
Frying, deep fat, Italian-style, 30

Lamb
  chops, Roman-style, 29
  roasted *capretto*, 28–29
Liver
  fried, Italian-style, 29–31
  sauce for *perciatelli*, 55
  Sicilian rice balls, 40
Lobster
  baked seafood Vesuvio, 23–24
  alla diavolo, 22

Melon with *prosciutto*, 13–14
Mushrooms
  batter fried, 31
  garnish for *saltimbocca*, 32
  in pizza topping, 62–63
  risotto Milanese, 39
  salad, 58–59
  Sicilian rice balls, 40
  on toast, 45–46

Olive oil, 57
Olive sauce for *ziti*, 56

Omelets
  fruit, 69, 71
  Italian-style, 36–37

Pasta
  basic preparation, 49–50
  bavette with meat sauce, 56
  fettucine, 50; with green noodles, 50
  four-faced (*quadrettini*), 54–55
  linguine with cauliflower sauce, 51;
    sailor-style, 56
  macaroni shells in onion sauce, 56
  mezzani, with eggplant, 55; with
    wine sauce, 56
  perciatelli, 55
  quills with herb butter, 56
  ravioli with cheese and oregano, 52
  rigati-sausage casserole, 56
  rigatoni, 55; with *pepperoni*, 56
  spaghetti *amatriciana*, 52–53; *alla
    carbonara*, 53; with garlic sauce, 55
  spinach macaroni with chili sauce, 56
  ziti, with olive sauce, 56; with
    ham sauce, 56
Peaches, baked Italienne, 72–73
Peas with *prosciutto*, 45
Peppers with anchovies, 12–13
Pine nuts, and rice, 38; and spinach, 46–47
Pizza
  basic dough recipe, 61
  calzoni, 64–65
  Margherita-style, 61–62
  Neapolitan *alla marinara*, 63–64
  toppings, 62–63
Potatoes
  new, with oregano, 46
  salad, Umbrian-style, 59–60
Prosciutto
  calzoni, 64
  four-faced pasta, 54–55
  with melons and figs, 13–14
  with mushrooms on toast, 46
  with peas, 45
  spaghetti *alla carbonara*, 53
  in veal dishes, 31, 33

Ricotta (cottage cheese), 42
  condita, 74
  Sicilian cream cheese cake, 73
  in Sicilian sandwich, 65–66

Rice
    balls, Roman-style, 38–39; Sicilian-style, 40
    minute, with spinach, 38–40
    with pine nuts, 38
    risotto, Milanese-style, 39
    stuffed tomatoes, 47–48

Salads
    cauliflower, 57–58
    chickpea, 10
    potato, Umbrian-style, 59–60
    raw mushroom, 58–59
    red kidney bean, 58; and tuna, 60
Sandwiches
    cheese in a carriage, 11–12
    crustini, 11
    hero, 65
    mushrooms on toast, 45–46
    Sicilian *guastiedde*, 65–66
Sauces for fish, 20–23; for meat, 9, 15, 20, 27; for pasta, 15–16, 50–56; for vegetables, 8–10
Sausage
    rigati casserole, 56
    rigatoni with pepperoni, 56
    sandwiches, 65–66
Seafood. *See* Fish and Seafood
Shrimp
    as pizza topping, 63
    scampi, Roman-style, 23; Venetian-style, 23
Soups
    fish stew, 17
    lemon and egg broth, 17
    minestrone, 16–17
    Pavese, 17–18
    pesto, 15–16
    stracciatella (little rag), 18
    zucchini, 17
Spinach
    baked eggs Florentine, 38
    four-faced pasta, 54–55
    with minute rice, 39
    omelet (*frittata maritate*), 36–37
    pasta, 50, 56
    with pine nuts and raisins, 46–47

Tangerines (oranges)
    fritters, 71
    frozen dessert, 73–74
Tomatoes
    pizza topping, 62–64
    salad, 31; with basil, 60
    sauces for pasta, 51–54
    stuffed, 13, 47–48
Tuna
    marinade for veal and poultry, 34–35
    spaghetti sauce, 54
Turkey, tunnied, 34

Veal
    cutlets, Bolognese, 33; *saltimbocca*, 31–32
    fillets with rosemary, 31
    osso buco, 34–35
    scalloppine alla marsala, 32–33
    stuffed pillows, 33–34
    tunnied, 34
Vegetables (raw), hot bath for, 8–9

Zucchini
    soup, 19
    straws, 48